THE VICTORIAN CEMETERY

Sarah Rutherford

SHIRE PUBLICATIONS

Published in Great Britain in 2010 by Shire Publications Ltd, Midland House, West Way, Botley, Oxford OX2 0PH, United Kingdom.
44-02 23rd St, Suite 219, Long Island City, NY 11101, USA.

E-mail: shire@shirebooks.co.uk   www.shirebooks.co.uk

© 2008 Sarah Rutherford; reprinted 2010.

All rights reserved. Apart from any fair dealing for the purpose of private study, research, criticism or review, as permitted under the Copyright, Designs and Patents Act, 1988, no part of this publication may be reproduced, stored in a retrieval system, or transmitted in any form or by any means, electronic, electrical, chemical, mechanical, optical, photocopying, recording or otherwise, without the prior written permission of the copyright owner. Enquiries should be addressed to the Publishers.

Every attempt has been made by the Publishers to secure the appropriate permissions for materials reproduced in this book. If there has been any oversight we will be happy to rectify the situation and a written submission should be made to the Publishers.

A CIP catalogue record for this book is available from the British Library.

Shire Library no. 481   •   ISBN-13: 978 0 74780 701 8

Sarah Rutherford has asserted her right under the Copyright, Designs and Patents Act, 1988, to be identified as the author of this book.

Designed by Ken Vail Graphic Design, Cambridge, UK and typeset in Perpetua and Gill Sans.
Printed in China through Worldprint.

10 11 12 13 14   11 10 9 8 7 6 5 4 3 2

COVER IMAGE
An angel monument in Brompton Cemetery, London. (Photograph by Ian Goulden.)

TITLE PAGE IMAGE
The Victorian cemetery was intended to be beautiful as well as practical. Utley Cemetery, West Yorkshire, opened in 1857, settles into a beautiful valley near Bradford. Its ornate monuments reflect the manufacturing dynasties of Victorian Keighley.

CONTENTS PAGE IMAGE
Barnsley Cemetery chapels, 1860.

ACKNOWLEDGEMENTS
Many people have patiently helped me to understand cemeteries and in the preparation of this book. I wish particularly to thank those who encouraged and advised me, including Jonathan Lovie, Julian Pooley of Surrey History Centre, Dr Brent Elliott, Dr Harriet Jordan, John Rotheroe, John Avery, and many members of the Friends of various cemeteries.

Illustrations are acknowledged as follows:

Brent Elliott, pages 3, 29, 30, 45 (top), 53 (top two), and 54 (top); British Association for Cemeteries in South Asia, page 9; Colin Clark, pages 26, 33, 46, and 51; English Heritage NMR, pages 8, 9, 20, 45 (bottom), and 49 (bottom right); Francis Frith, page 16; Friends of Arnos Vale Cemetery, page 19; Guildhall Library City of London, pages 14, 17, 35 (top), and 36; The Kent Messenger Group, page 61; Lens of Sutton Collection, pages 55 and 56; Jonathan Lovie 14, 15, 18 (top left), 32 (bottom right), 43 (bottom), and 54 (bottom); Museum of London, page 12; and Jenifer White, page 11.

Other illustrations are taken from contemporary publications, the source being identified in the caption, or are photographs by the author.

Shire Publications is supporting the Woodland Trust, the UK's leading woodland conservation charity, by funding the dedication of trees.

CONTENTS

INTRODUCTION: ELYSIAN FIELDS	5
ORIGINS	8
CREATING THE GARDEN CEMETERY	13
JOHN CLAUDIUS LOUDON	24
THE GREAT GARDEN OF DEATH, 1850–1901	31
PARADISE PRESERVED? THE CEMETERIES TODAY	58
FURTHER READING	61
PLACES TO VISIT	63
INDEX	64

INTRODUCTION: ELYSIAN FIELDS

'A cemetery can and should, by the exercise of art, be made as beautiful as possible.' H. E. Milner, *The Art and Practice of Landscape Gardening*, 1890.

A cemetery is a place for burials, other than a churchyard or graveyard attached to a regular place of worship. Cemeteries are usually multi-denominational but may belong exclusively to a single denomination.

This definition conveys no idea of the richness and variety of cemeteries, their place at the heart of a long-lost cult of death and mourning, nor their importance as a nineteenth-century phenomenon. They were one of many institutions developed as essential parts of Victorian society: from workhouses, asylums and prisons to public parks and boarding schools. Although in some ways the cemetery was a typical Victorian institution, well regulated and with a defined structure, in other ways it was unique. It was a new type of burial ground for the dead, bringing innovation in the assemblage of landscape design, architecture, planting and social use, and became a countrywide asset.

Few suitable models were obvious for the Victorian cemetery. Before the nineteenth century the most likely model, the Anglican parish churchyard, had been the burial ground for most people. After 1800, in the many growing urban areas, churchyards quickly filled and were seen as inefficient, unhygienic and unpleasant verging on the horrific. A new type of landscape was required to bury the dead according to the prevailing social and sanitary needs – one that was not necessarily attached to a place of worship, but that could accommodate religious rites of all sorts. Garden cemeteries were developed, at first by private companies and later by public authorities, to make the most dignified and efficient use of the land. They were traversed by roads and paths to give access to chapels and burial plots. Their layout modified the eighteenth-century style of Arcadian pleasure ground used for the country-house estate and for public pleasure gardens where people enjoyed walks and entertainment in sylvan surroundings. They were usually divided religiously into sections dedicated to various denominations, and socially by sections dictated by the price of the grave plot.

Opposite: Hundreds of provincial public cemeteries were established and the scale, design and quality of buildings usually reflected a high degree of civic pride. This is the plan by H. E. Milner for Stoke-on-Trent Cemetery, Staffordshire, designed c. 1884 and published in 1890. This late layout reflected the earliest 'Pleasure Ground' type of layout and planting of the 1830s and 1840s, of which Loudon disapproved. (from *The Art and Practice of Landscape Gardening*, H. E. Milner 1890)

THE VICTORIAN CEMETERY

Victorian cemeteries were great social levellers, where people of all classes were buried and their friends and relations met frequently. Each was open to the whole community, focused on one, two or occasionally three chapels. These stood at the heart of tranquil, attractive grounds, calm in character to soothe mourning visitors and provide a contemplative pointer to Paradise. Cemeteries spread countrywide, and their number grew rapidly during Queen Victoria's reign (1837–1901).

The spiritual character of the Victorian cemetery was epitomised by two places that were evoked in the layout. Paradoxically, these derive from ancient classical sources rather than Christian. Arcadia was a mountainous and picturesque district of Greece, in the heart of the Peloponnesus, whose people were distinguished for contentment and rural happiness. This was translated into the eighteenth-century English landscape garden as a scene of simple rural pleasure and untroubled quiet. Elysium was the ancient Greek dwelling place assigned to happy souls favoured by the gods after death; it was the seat of future happiness, Paradise. The Elysian Fields were the abode of the blessed after death. The Victorian cemetery sought to mirror Elysium by creating an Arcadian setting for the mortal remains of the deceased: man's idea of Paradise on earth.

Interest in Victorian cemeteries waned in the twentieth century as mortality became more remote from everyday life. They have become consistently underrated for their visual and architectural qualities and

The Wood family mausoleum amongst mourning evergreens in the Anglican section at Brookwood Cemetery, Surrey. It resembled an ancient Roman temple, evoking classical Arcadian associations.

contribution to the quality of life. Fortunately, interest is growing again, prompted by thriving studies in family history, by the threats from a recurring acute need for more burial space, and by an appreciation of their value as cultural landscapes and ornamental open spaces. The Victorian core of our cemeteries is by now usually full and redundant, sometimes isolated where extension was not possible, or else ringed by later additions of land for burials. Many Victorian cemeteries are closed to burials after a century or more of service. Others continue to serve our needs for an Arcadian setting for our deceased loved ones. In either case they remain essential features of our culture and lives.

Several terms require brief explanation:

Protestant: a Christian who rejects the authority of the Roman Catholic Church.

Anglican: the national and established Church of England, which is Protestant.

Nonconformist or Dissenter: a Protestant who does not conform to the disciplines or rites of the Anglican Church, including Methodists, Congregationalists and Quakers.

Tunbridge Wells Cemetery, Kent, opened in 1849. It is now full and has suffered from some neglect, but, with its modest chapel (red), serpentine layout of drives (brown) and paths (orange), hilly site and collections of fine trees and memorials, it is valued by the residents as a great asset to their town. The local authority and Friends Group are working together to ensure it has a secure future in this role.

ORIGINS

Before the nineteenth century the dead were usually interred in consecrated parish churchyards, where their burial was the responsibility of the Church of England. Wealthier parishioners had the option of burial in vaults sunk into the church floor. However, in Anglican consecrated ground the parish priest was obliged to conduct the burial service from the Book of Common Prayer, and other denominations and religions were forbidden to conduct funerals there.

The earliest burial grounds outside parish churchyards appeared from the 1650s as a response to the exclusion of non-Anglicans from churchyards. These were the modest and utilitarian forerunners of the Victorian cemetery. Their numbers were small, with a concentration around London. They served other denominations or religions, such as the Nonconformist burial ground at Bunhill Fields, London, and the Jewish burial grounds in the East End. Several of the latter were established, including those in Alderney Road, Whitechapel (1697; $1\frac{1}{4}$ acres), Brady Street (1761; 5 acres), Lauriston Road (1788; $2\frac{1}{2}$ acres), and farther afield and slightly later in Fulham (1815;

The Quaker Burial Ground, Jordans, Buckinghamshire, dates from the seventeenth century. The simple grass plot laid out in a grid with plain headstones is one of the earliest Dissenters' burial grounds. William Penn's grave is on the left, front row.

Eighteenth-century memorials in South Park Street Cemetery, Calcutta. One of the earliest garden cemeteries, it was founded in 1767, predating European burial reform, and became filled with many spectacular memorials before it closed in the 1830s.

A number of Jewish burial grounds were opened in the eighteenth century. Penzance Jewish Cemetery is one of the best-preserved Georgian Jewish burial grounds in Britain. This gravestone commemorates Jacob James Hart.

1¼ acres), which, as Hugh Meller says, is more typical of Jewish cemeteries in Prague than those in London.

Burial grounds were not restricted to London. The early Quaker meeting house at Jordans, Buckinghamshire (1688), stood in a small ground, where plots were arranged in a grid pattern with headstones of characteristically simple design. They include the modest grave of William Penn (died 1718), one of the founding fathers of the United States, after whom the state of Pennsylvania was named. The land for the Jewish cemetery in Exeter was leased from the city council as early as 1757 and that on the Hoe at Plymouth was begun around the same time.

As the Industrial Revolution took hold, urban populations rose massively, particularly in London. Urban parish churchyards were put under great pressure to take burials, even when full, leading to unsanitary conditions and the spread of disease. The ancient Roman idea of locating burials and cemeteries on the edge of towns was revived from the seventeenth century onwards, promoted by notable architects and thinkers such as Sir Christopher Wren, John Evelyn and Sir John Vanbrugh. Wren and Evelyn both advised that large cemeteries should be formed outside the City of London after the Great Fire of 1666, but this did not occur.

During the eighteenth century a cemetery movement was developing worldwide. A grand cemetery for Europeans was founded at South Park Street, Calcutta, in 1767 and became filled with spectacular memorials, including rotundas, obelisks, pyramids and truncated columns. It was at the

Some of the earliest garden cemeteries in the United States were laid out in the southern states. New Orleans Lafayette No. 1 has an urban street character, derived from the mausolea. Burials below ground were not possible because of the high water table.

forefront of burial reform and was one of the first of many subsequently created in south Asia. In North America, cemeteries developed in French Louisiana in the far south. By 1725 New Orleans had a cemetery outside the city and in the late eighteenth century the St Louis Cemetery was established there, with above-ground tombs built to avoid contamination from flooding of the swampy ground. These were the beginnings of the great cemeteries that continued to be built in the city and survive today.

The first urban cemeteries in the British Isles were also created in the eighteenth century. They, too, lay outside England, including in 1718 one in Edinburgh on Calton Hill, and in 1797 the old Clifton Street Cemetery in Belfast. This British precedent provided the framework for solving the problems both of overcrowded churchyards, and of providing burial space for various Christian denominations and other religions, until now catered for only by the Anglican churchyards and the scattered, small burial grounds. Architectural ornament, sometimes of an extremely high quality, made a great contribution to these early cemeteries. The great Scots neo-classical architect Robert Adam designed the monument to the philosopher David Hume at Calton Hill (1777). Here, as in New Orleans, the tombs were set closely together, creating the effect of urban streets with houses on either side.

George Frederick Carden in the 1820s in *The Penny Magazine* was one of the first to suggest public cemeteries in England in the nineteenth century, drawn from European and American precedent. He compared the 'abodes of the dead in France, Spain, Germany, and in the principal States of America' with Britain's 'hideous burial-grounds'. These new cemeteries were 'open and airy spaces, mostly decent, frequently beautiful', and often 'formed the favourite places of resort for the neighbouring population'.

Inspiration for the great Victorian garden cemetery in Britain came particularly from one example in Paris, the Cimetière du Père-Lachaise, opened in 1804. Ironically, this was at the height of the Napoleonic Wars with France, although the design model was the English landscape park. At Père-Lachaise these landscaping ideas were developed to create an attractive answer to the city's burial needs. It was built on picturesquely hilly ground. Axial avenues were softened by winding paths, flowing ground and landscape planting of clumps of trees and shrubs. But the aesthetic of its Elysian landscaping was based upon a sound economic proposition that offered burial plots for sale in perpetuity as well as an asset for the community. The cemetery was segregated socially by price of plots, so ensuring that civic rank would be maintained forever, even in death, an idea enthusiastically taken up in British cemeteries. These social divisions were often expressed physically by impressive and expensive monuments. Those who could not afford perpetuity could purchase a five-year lease on a plot; paupers were buried in common graves that each contained seven corpses.

Père-Lachaise Cemetery, Paris, opened in 1804, was a highly influential Arcadian model for Victorian garden cemeteries in Britain.

CREATING THE GARDEN CEMETERY

'A garden cemetery and monumental decoration afford the most convincing token of a nation's progress in civilisation and the arts, which are its result.'
John Strang, *Necropolis Glasguensis*, 1831.

THE earliest English garden cemeteries were set up primarily for religious motives rather than reasons of health. The first cemetery in England, the Rosary in Norwich, was set up by a dissenting clergyman, Thomas Drummond, in 1819, using his own money. It was non-denominational and its 5 acres offered space to Nonconformists and Anglicans alike, a great innovation. Shortly after this, in the 1820s, several cemeteries were established in the north of England by Nonconformists as an alternative to Anglican parish churchyards, including two in Manchester, one in Liverpool (Low Hill), and Westgate Hill Cemetery in Newcastle upon Tyne (1825).

Liverpool was among the first English cities to establish a garden cemetery. In 1829 St James's Cemetery was opened as a commercial venture to cater for Anglicans by a joint-stock company. This was a business whose capital was held in transferable shares of stock by its joint owners (in effect falling between a partnership and a corporation). It cost £21,000 and occupied around 12 acres. By 1830 it was so successful that it was providing an annual dividend of 8 per cent. The landscape design was of key importance in attracting customers, and the cemetery was later described by Nikolaus Pevsner as the most romantic in England. Entrances, carriage ramps and buildings were designed by the Liverpool architect John Foster (1787–1846), who was also the architect for the Nonconformist Low Hill. The landscaping was by John Shepherd, curator of the Liverpool Botanic Garden.

The design of St James's made dramatic use of a quarry site. Its two main buildings were designed in neo-classical style and placed strategically for most impact (but not for convenient direct access to graves): a lodge to the south, and the oratory chapel to the north. Built on higher ground above the quarry floor and the grave plots, at the head of sandstone cliffs, these occupied the sites of former windmills. A series of ramps led up the quarry

Opposite: Kensal Green Cemetery, opened in 1833, was the first of London's nineteenth-century commercial public cemeteries to be established, to a design by Richard Forrest. Its neo-classical buildings and sinuous layout of paths were enclosed by a high wall.

THE VICTORIAN CEMETERY

One of the first garden cemeteries was provincial. St James's, Liverpool, was opened in 1829 in a former quarry next to the site of the present Anglican cathedral. The architect was John Foster, with landscaping by his associate John Shepherd. Great ramps led to the floor of the quarry, with catacombs cut into the sides. Ornament was important to attract clients.

By 1830 a solution to London's burial needs was sought. Francis Goodwin designed an ambitious and fanciful proposal for a vast, monumental Grand National Cemetery intended for Primrose Hill, London, above Regent's Park.

face, with vaults set into the rocky bank where they required no drainage and, as the writer and landscape designer John Claudius Loudon remarked approvingly, could be entered without descending more than a few steps. The design emphasised enclosure, which became a major element in English cemetery design over the next two decades.

By 1830 mortality rates in cities were horrifying and the idea of the cemetery, detached from a permanent place of worship, was being discussed more seriously. It would solve the problem of overcrowded churchyards by being set beyond the urban centre, allowing spacious and long-term provision. In most cases it would cater for all denominations and sometimes other religions, taking over from the small burial grounds, by being split into consecrated and unconsecrated sections (for Anglicans and others, respectively). Ambitious schemes began to appear for London. A proposal for a Grand National Cemetery was put forward in 1830 by the architect Francis Goodwin (1784–1835), who had a successful church-building practice, for

CREATING THE GARDEN CEMETERY

Key Hill Cemetery, Birmingham, opened in 1836 and was set in a former quarry.

a 150-acre site at Primrose Hill, above Regent's Park in London. The outer area was 'disposed somewhat after the manner of Père la Chaise' at Paris, and an inner enclosure contained temples and mausolea, which were to be 'facsimiles of some of the celebrated remains of Greek and Roman architecture' (*Gentleman's Magazine*, 1830). At its centre stood a great Greek-style temple and the whole vast area was to be enclosed by miles of colonnades, guarded by lodges and overlooked by a memorial column. The plan was never realised and in any case was always more of an idealised Elysian concept than a practical scheme.

During the 1830s further commercial cemeteries were set up, based on the financially advantageous joint-stock model. Thus commercial enterprise set the pattern that was used as the model for later public cemeteries. Because the cemetery was a place for permanent and public commemoration and would be a focal point for the cult of commemoration, it was important, when combined with commercial needs, to create an attractive environment that would win customers in a competitive market. These cemeteries were generally set up in regional centres, including Key Hill, Birmingham (opened 1836, 7 acres, also within a former quarry); Newcastle General (set up 1834; 8 acres); Sheffield General (1836, 5 acres); Manchester General (opened 1837, 12 acres); York Public (1837, 7 acres);

York Cemetery was designed by James Pigott Pritchett and opened in 1837. The Greek Revival-style chapel stands between the consecrated and unconsecrated ground, and the interior, similarly, is partly consecrated.

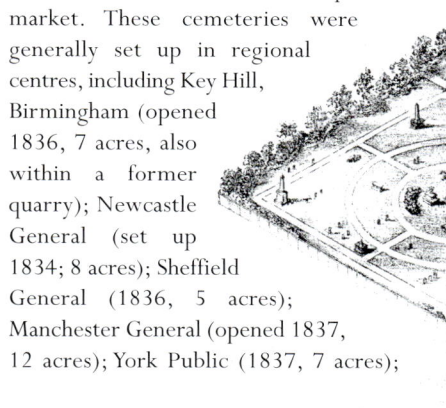

Glasgow Necropolis opened in 1832 and became the most spectacular cemetery in Britain. This photograph, taken in 1897, shows it as 'a dream-like vision of Attic splendour'.

Nottingham General (1837–40, 14 acres); Gravesend (set up 1838, 5½ acres, re-using an unsuccessful former public pleasure garden); and Arnos Vale, Bristol (opened 1840, about 30 acres). At York Cemetery it cost £4,400 to lay out the grounds and construct the two cemetery buildings (the chapel and lodge) and the railings and gate, and just under £2,000 for the 7-acre site, a total of £6,400. It was calculated that, with grave plots measuring 7 feet 6 inches by 3 feet, this would provide just over 15,500 burial spaces, considered adequate for the burial needs of the city for over ninety years.

Elsewhere in the British Isles, the Glasgow Necropolis opened in 1832. This was inspired by the publication in 1831 of *Necropolis Glasguensis*, a seminal work by the Scot John Strang aimed at forming a large commercial cemetery on a hill in Glasgow next to the cathedral. The Necropolis was the first major cemetery in Scotland and, as Curl put it, 'There can be no cemetery in Britain as spectacular as the Glasgow Necropolis ... a dream-like vision of Attic splendour, on a hill beside the cathedral'. In the same year Mount Prospect Cemetery was founded at Glasnevin in Dublin. Mount Auburn Cemetery, Cambridge, Massachusetts (1831), was one of the first landscaped cemeteries in the United States, created as 'a rural cemetery and experimental garden'.

Meanwhile London, the greatest capital city in the world, lagged behind the provinces and other capital cities in its cemetery provision. Its first proper cemetery was not opened until 1832, and even then it was left to private enterprise to pioneer this essential sanitary measure in the capital. In the first fifty years of the nineteenth century London's population more than doubled from 1 million to 2.3 million, and the problem of safe burial became acute. In 1831 the first great cholera epidemic occurred and it was believed

CREATING THE GARDEN CEMETERY

The striking catacombs at Highgate Cemetery, London, enclosed the 'Circle of Lebanon', a sunken ring of tombs around a cedar tree remaining from the garden previously on the site.

(wrongly) that the disease was spread by the evil-smelling miasmas that arose from the overcrowded burial grounds, rather than by contaminated water. Fortuitously, this mistaken belief spurred action in the right direction. In 1832 a Bill was passed for 'establishing a General Cemetery for the Interment of the Dead in the Neighbourhood of the Metropolis'. A group of London cemeteries developed that followed the commercial model established by Père-Lachaise. The first was Kensal Green, opened in 1833 by the General Cemetery Company, and still under its management. It was another five years before the next was set up – as the South Metropolitan Cemetery, West Norwood, founded in 1836, which for many years was the most fashionable London cemetery south of the river. There followed Nunhead Cemetery, opened in 1840 to serve the area south of the Thames; Highgate (1839) and Abney Park, Stoke Newington (1840), for the north; Brompton Cemetery (1840) for the west; and Tower Hamlets (1841), for the east. It had taken

Tower Hamlets Cemetery was one of London's 'Magnificent Seven' cemeteries, laid out before the Burial Acts of the 1850s: an engraving of 1841.

17

St Bartholomew's Cemetery, Exeter, opened in 1837. Unusually, the cemetery was designed without chapels. The Egyptian-style catacombs at the heart of the layout were for 22,000 bodies. The cemetery closed when full in 1874, but the catacombs remained unfilled, reflecting changing burial fashions.

nearly a decade for this 'Magnificent Seven' to make adequate provision for London, but even these quickly became inadequate, so rapidly was London continuing to expand.

Publicly funded cemeteries remained rare until the 1850s Burial Acts, indicating that legislation was necessary to encourage the provision of new cemeteries available to all denominations and classes. Exeter Cemetery was the first cemetery in England paid for by public money, being funded from the rates; it remained the only one in the 1830s funded by this means. In a pioneering corporate move to improve urban sanitary conditions during the 1840s following the passing of the Leeds Burial Act of 1842, Leeds City Corporation opened three cemeteries, at Armley, Holbeck and Burmantofts (Beckett Street, opened in 1845). The total cost was £25,000. Over 180,000 people were interred at Beckett Street in some 28,000 graves. Southampton Corporation used part of the Common as a cemetery, opened in 1846 following a private parliamentary bill introduced in 1843.

These cemeteries were generally set in rural areas on the outskirts of the town, on cheap land, initially with room for expansion. The picturesque treatment of the layout, exemplified at Père-Lachaise, was an important part of the scheme, whether the cemetery was run for commercial profit or by the authorities, and so the 'garden cemetery' was born. It was intended to be a 'gateway to Heaven', to conduct the interment of the deceased, and a rural Arcadia to house their remains, where friends and relatives could visit their memorials as often as they wished in an attractive and evocative setting. In rural areas, churchyards continued to cater for Anglican parishioners and some Nonconformist congregations created burial grounds adjacent to their own chapels.

The attractiveness of a hilly site such as at Père-Lachaise was not just visual, but economic. Land that had little other value, and was thus cheap, could be used. Quarry sites were selected for St James's, Liverpool, and Key Hill, Birmingham, and were used for several other cemeteries, despite the difficulties of burying in rocky terrain. The steeply sloping sites of Highgate, London (1839), and Glasgow Necropolis (1832) provided both interesting relief and spectacular views of their respective metropolises. In other sites on more level ground paths curved through informal lawns destined for graves and monuments and planted with ornamental and native trees. Often the design was focused or hinged on a formal feature such as a viewing terrace, as at the circular catacombs terrace at Highgate, or more often on an axial carriage avenue giving access to chapels, such as at Nunhead, Gravesend and Reading, where curving paths led off the main drive. A few were entirely based on a grid pattern, such as the spectacular one at Brompton, London (1840).

Notable designers, usually landscapers or architects or a combination of both, were employed on prestigious commissions to lay out various cemeteries. The landscape designer Stephen Geary planned Highgate (opened 1839) in part and Gravesend (1838) and submitted an unsuccessful design for Brompton in 1837 with the landscaper David Ramsay. The architect John Dobson laid out Newcastle General Cemetery (opened 1836), to an acclaimed design. In 1840 the architect James Bunstone Bunning, surveyor for the London Cemetery Company, designed a layout for a cemetery on Nunhead Hill, near Peckham. The architect Benjamin Baud (who had unsuccessfully submitted designs for the Houses of Parliament in 1835) designed the unremittingly formal Anglican Brompton Cemetery, where work began in 1839.

Some cemeteries, such as Highgate in London, Gravesend in Kent and Arnos Vale, Bristol (laid out 1837–40), were created on the site of earlier gardens and incorporated earlier landscaping.

A strong element of civic pride prevailed, and a note of competition between towns is evident. At Arnos Vale the idea of creating an Arcadian garden as the last resting place for Bristol citizens was enthusiastically received. *Felix Farley's Bristol Journal* reported in October 1840 upon the opening of the cemetery, which was a popular event, attended on a beautiful autumn morning by 'a large concourse of spectators including our resident fashionables'. It went on to say that 'We think that we may in all safety predict, when all arrangements are completed, the grounds planted, the various tombs and memorials erected, that few if any cemeteries in the kingdom will surpass the Cemetery at Arnos Vale.'

The range of buildings in these early commercial cemeteries set the pattern for later examples. Typically, an impressive

THE VICTORIAN CEMETERY

The tomb, or *chattri*, of Raja Rammouhun Roy Bahadoor, in Arnos Vale Cemetery, Bristol, was built of Bath stone and designed by William Princep. The celebrated Indian reformer and philosopher died in 1833 while on a brief visit to Bristol. The non conformist chapel in the distance was designed by Charles Underwood in classical Greek Ionic style.

entrance combining lodge, offices and gateway opened on to the drive to the single chapel or pair of chapels. At this early stage in the development of the cemetery, most were based on the classical neo-Greek style, such as the two at Arnos Vale (see previous page), although latterly a few were Gothic, and the lodges, chapel and gateway at Highgate were designed by Geary in Tudor style. A monumental Egyptian Revival appeared in some places, including the catacombs at Highgate and St Bartholomew's, Exeter (1837). But by the 1850s, following the Gothic Revival in architecture, it was accepted that Gothic was the 'correct' style for a Christian cemetery and nearly all

Right and opposite: Several ranges of catacombs were provided by the company at the Plymouth, Stonehouse and Devonport Cemetery (laid out in 1847–8, now known as Ford Park Cemetery), where they were unusually popular.

CREATING THE GARDEN CEMETERY

cemetery buildings were built in this style from then onwards.

The gateway was a key feature heralding the entrance to Elysium, which also happened to be a prestigious place of commemoration. More practically, this 'gateway to Heaven' housed the lodge-keeper and cemetery office, with one or two lodges or a gateway with flanking lodges in the style of a triumphal arch. Arnos Vale has two lodges in the form of classical temples flanking the gateway; Kensal Green, Sheffield General and Reading have imposing classical archways. At Nunhead, Bunning designed a dignified entrance with four monolithic Portland-stone piers decorated with symbols of death: inverted torches in cast iron, and iron wreaths on the square terminals above, all linked by cast-iron railings and gates. Abney Park, Stoke Newington, had single-storey lodges and piers in the form of Egyptian pylons. The architect, William Hosking, was aided by Joseph Bonomi junior, who provided the hieroglyphic inscription for the lodges, which announced 'The Gates of the Abode of the Mortal Part of Man'. Mount Auburn, Cambridge, Massachusetts, also had an Egyptian-style gateway joined to flanking lodges. An unusual water gate in Gothic style was proposed (but never constructed) for Kensal Green Cemetery, leading off the adjacent Paddington Canal and complementing the more conventional carriage gateway on the other side of the site. Cemeteries were closed at night and surrounded by high walls or iron railings to prevent unauthorised entry, theft and vandalism.

The catacombs at Highgate were the prestigious focus of the design, attracting those who visited. (*The Mirror*, November 1838.)

Highgate Cemetery, the third private cemetery on the fringe of London, opened in 1839. This is the dramatic Egyptian-style entrance to the catacombs, around the Lebanon Circle.

The focal point of the cemetery was the chapel or pair of chapels in which committal services were conducted by the priest or minister before the interment took place. Each chapel provided for services for the allocated denomination only, but without giving preferential treatment to either. Where the cemetery provided both for Anglicans (with consecrated ground) and Nonconformists (unconsecrated), they were always buried separately in two sections, often divided by a wall or marker stones, such as at Exeter and Reading, each with its own chapel standing separately in its respective section. The axial carriage drive might act as the division between the two sections and sometimes led directly from the main gate to the Anglican chapel, indicating that this was the most important denomination in the cemetery, as at Kensal Green, Nunhead, Gravesend and Reading. Other denominations were served in the Dissenters' sections, and in the Glasgow Necropolis the first burial in the cemetery was of a Jew, Joseph Levi, a jeweller, in 1832. The neo-Greek classical style in various types was popular in the 1830s for chapels. At Kensal Green the Anglican chapel was in Greek Doric style and the Dissenters' chapel in Ionic. West Norwood (South Metropolitan Cemetery, 1837) had the first cemetery buildings erected in the Gothic style (by William Tite), and from this time the classical style declined rapidly as the dominant style in favour of Gothic.

The other main structure sometimes constructed was the catacombs: sunken or underground burial galleries with recesses in their sides for tombs, drawing on an antique Roman model. A premium could be asked for burial in these more prestigious galleries, which were usually of considerable architectural note. At Highgate a circular avenue was built into the hillside in Egyptian style in a ring around a symbolic cedar of Lebanon, with a monumental gateway in the same style. A series of doorways led into the individual burial chambers. This was later imitated at Glasnevin in Dublin.

The great range of underground catacombs below the Anglican chapel at Kensal Green was brick-vaulted with individual cells leading off the passageways. A novel device, a specially constructed hydraulic coffin lift or catafalque, still descends to the vaults. At St Bartholemew's, Exeter the catacombs, also Egyptian in style, ran along a terrace at the top of the hillside overlooking the rest of the cemetery below and the valley opposite, with the vaults set into the hillside and entered through large doors. At Key Hill, Birmingham, circular catacombs were set into the rising ground, with a curving rock face and brick wall. These were apparently a successful venture and were extended in several phases in the 1850s and 1860s. Above, a platform and promenade provided views to the countryside beyond the city. At Gravesend the catacombs were designed to take five hundred coffins. Their construction used up a substantial amount of the capital; by 1838 work on them had been halted, to the annoyance of their architect, Geary, and they were never completed. By the mid-nineteenth century catacombs were less fashionable and the catacombs at Gravesend proved a financial failure, although ranges were built in nine London cemeteries at this time.

The initially open grassy and treed spaces were intended to be filled with monuments to line the paths and drives and complement the architecture of the chapels and lodges. The areas adjacent to the main drives and chapels were the most expensive plots and attracted prestigious families and their high-quality monuments. Kensal Green even attracted royalty in its early days: in front of the Anglican chapel is the polished slab to Augustus Frederick, Duke of Sussex, sixth son of George III and one of Queen Victoria's many uncles. His burial here in 1843 gave the cemetery immense prestige and added to its prosperity, as did that of his sister, Princess Sophia, who died in 1848 and was commemorated by an impressive Renaissance sarcophagus.

Glasnevin Cemetery, Dublin, opened in 1832, has become the largest cemetery in Ireland. The later catacombs were sunken and circular, similar to Highgate, London, which may have influenced them.

JOHN CLAUDIUS LOUDON

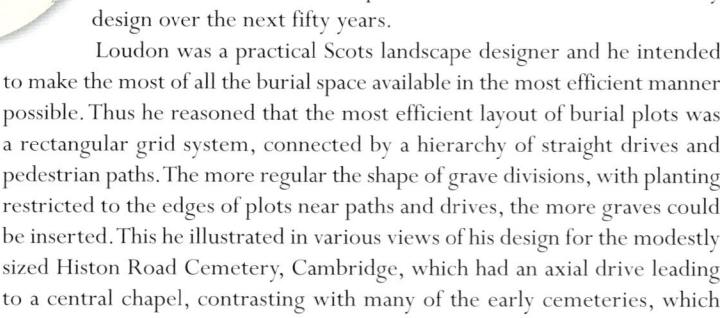

JOHN CLAUDIUS LOUDON (1783–1843) was a major influence on cemetery designers for the rest of the nineteenth century through a detailed account of his experience and views in *On the Laying Out, Planting and Managing of Cemeteries* (1843). This was influenced by Strang's 1831 *Necropolis Glasguensis*. Loudon tackled all aspects of the subject, from the design, layout and appropriate planting of the site to efficient grave-digging, vault construction and book-keeping. Loudon did not shrink from his self-imposed duty to attend to even the most gruesome detail if it was likely to improve the efficient and hygienic disposal of the dead. Although he died in the same year that the book was published and never witnessed the major cemetery-building boom, he had, nevertheless, substantial posthumous influence on cemetery design over the next fifty years.

Loudon was a practical Scots landscape designer and he intended to make the most of all the burial space available in the most efficient manner possible. Thus he reasoned that the most efficient layout of burial plots was a rectangular grid system, connected by a hierarchy of straight drives and pedestrian paths. The more regular the shape of grave divisions, with planting restricted to the edges of plots near paths and drives, the more graves could be inserted. This he illustrated in various views of his design for the modestly sized Histon Road Cemetery, Cambridge, which had an axial drive leading to a central chapel, contrasting with many of the early cemeteries, which had curving paths and drives between the blocks of plots. Only where the site was hilly did he abandon his rigid grid system, recommending broad sweeps

John Claudius Loudon (1783–1843), the doyen of cemetery design.

Grave boards were used while digging a grave to shape and retain the walls. (J. C. Loudon, *On the Laying Out of Cemeteries*, 1843.)

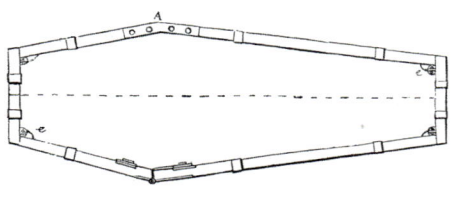

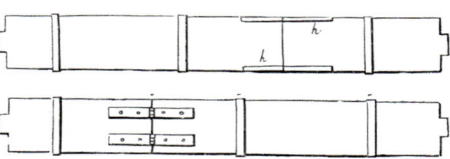

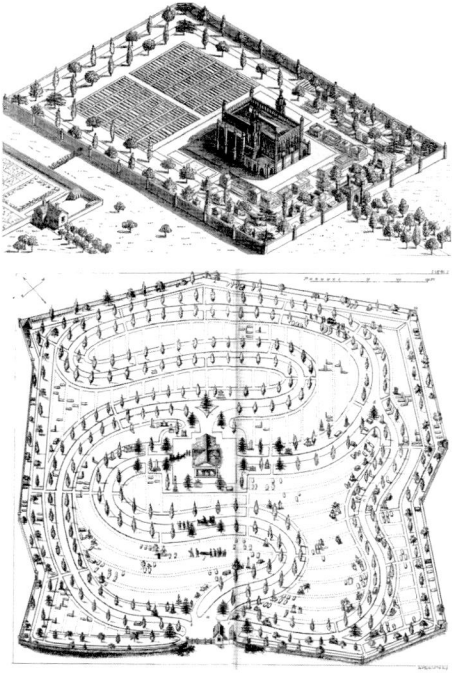 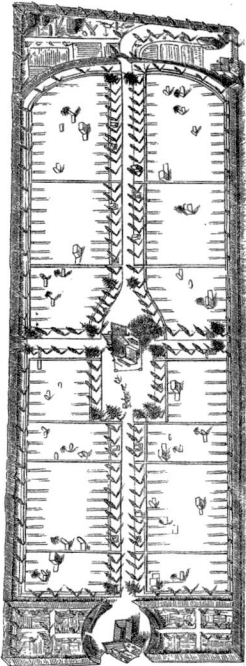

Top left: Loudon's design for a modest cemetery for an agricultural parish. The grid pattern made best use of space and was ornamented with many upright and evergreen trees along the perimeter path to ensure that little burial space was lost to planting.

Left: Loudon's simple Histon Road Cemetery, Cambridge, was one of three of his designs that were implemented, the others being Southampton and Bath Abbey.

Lower far left: Loudon's design for laying out and planting a cemetery on hilly ground departed from his usual regular grid. In order to accommodate the gradients for hearses and mourners, the paths traversed the slope of the site, ornamented with avenues of upright evergreens, probably Irish yew. (J. C. Loudon, *On the Laying Out of Cemeteries*, 1843.)

to ease the gradients, and so producing a more relaxed layout. This too he illustrated, but in a design that was apparently not executed. He recommended that 1,361 graves per acre were sufficient, given a death rate of 3 per cent per annum. Thus an acre would suffice for a population of one thousand for forty-five years. With the population of London at 1.5 million, this would require 33 acres per annum.

The shareholders perceived that a grand cemetery would attract a higher (and therefore more wealthy) class of clientele, and so the control and selection of those who entered the cemetery was important. For a populous neighbourhood, Loudon recommended a boundary wall 10 to 12 feet high. Panels of iron railings inserted in the wall at intervals would give visitors and passers-by pleasant views into and out of the cemetery. This would enhance the cemetery's reputation as a place of repose and contemplative resort of some social standing.

It must have a main gate and lodge, where a gatekeeper lived and could ensure that only the right sort of people entered. The lodge should never be 'mistaken either for an entrance to a public park or to a country residence'. It was also the administrative hub of the cemetery, for it would have 'a room to serve as an office to contain the cemetery books, or at least the order book

THE VICTORIAN CEMETERY

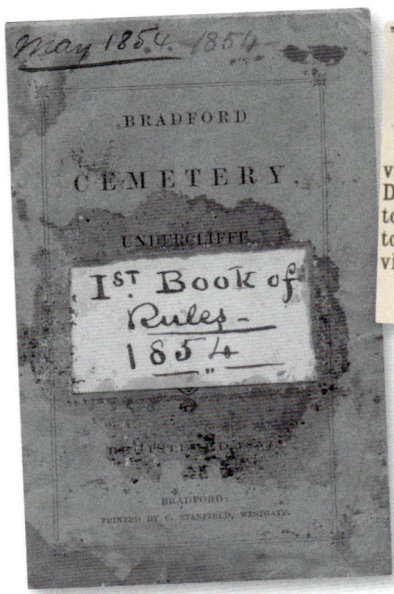

Left:
Cemeteries, like all other Victorian institutions, had rules to ensure appropriate behaviour and prohibit abuse. This is the *First Book of Rules* for Undercliffe Cemetery, Bradford.

Above:
Stealing floral decorations from graves was not unknown. This notice at Undercliffe Cemetery, Bradford, shows that a considerable reward was offered, when an average weekly wage was less than £1.

Few cemeteries were publicly funded before the 1850s. Leeds Corporation Cemetery, Beckett Street, opened in 1845, was an early example. This mid-nineteenth-century Ordnance Survey plan shows Loudon's favoured grid pattern of paths. The chapels stood near the entrances to the respective Anglican and Nonconformist sections.

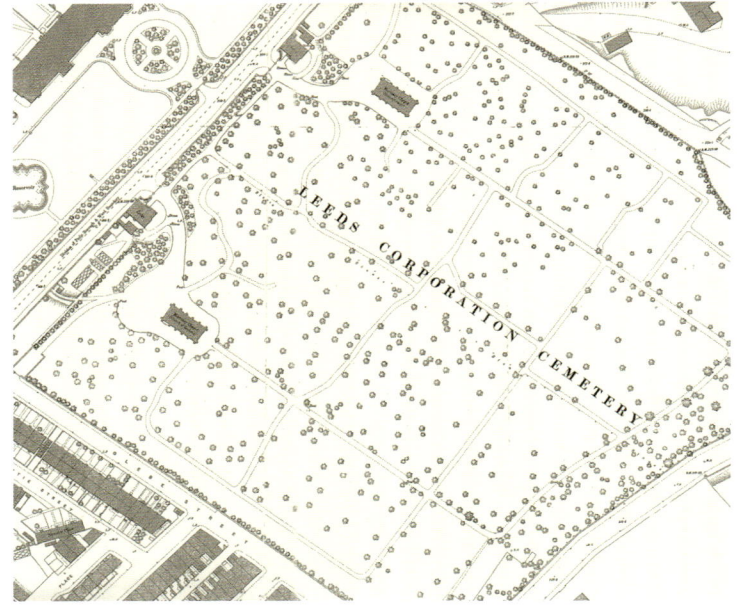

and register, and the map book, where for the system of squares being employed, such a book is rendered necessary'. The need for a good cemetery 'curator', who would oversee all this, was pivotal. He should be 'a man of intelligence and of cultivated feelings, with a taste for and some knowledge of gardening; for all which reasons ... the situation [was] one well adapted for a middle-aged gardener.'

To achieve easy circulation around a cemetery to all plots, he recommended a hierarchy of roads and paths: the roads being from 12 to 20 feet wide, according to the size of the cemetery; subsidiary walks not less than 5 to 6 feet wide; and so-called 'green paths' of 3 to 4 feet width between rows of plots. The practical reason was so that 'a funeral may be performed in any part of the grounds, or a grave in any part of the grounds visited, without once deviating from these paths, or treading on any graves'. Never one to ignore detail, he also addressed the need for service yards for grave-digging and horticultural activities, including the provision of sheds and glasshouses.

The chapels were to be placed in a 'central and conspicuous situation, so as, if possible, to be seen from all the prominent points of view along the roads and walks'. If more than one chapel was provided, they should be either grouped conspicuously together to appear as one building, or placed so far apart that they could not be seen from the same point. Catacombs above ground were in 'bad taste'.

Right:
Drives were carefully designed so that vehicles, particularly horse-drawn hearses, could move freely from the cemetery entrance to chapels and interment plots. A hearse and mourners at a mid-nineteenth-century funeral at Highgate Cemetery, London.

Below:
A truck hearse made for a less expensive funeral, being pulled by men rather than horses.
(J. C. Loudon, *On the Laying Out of Cemeteries*, 1843.)

Loudon contrasted the 'Pleasure Ground' planting style (left), which he disapproved of, and the 'Cemetery' style (right), which he promoted. The Cemetery style used many evergreens and fastigiate trees alongside paths and drives, rather than scattered clumps with spreading habits on open areas of burial plots. This is the South Metropolitan Cemetery, West Norwood, Surrey. (J. C. Loudon, *On the Laying Out of Cemeteries*, 1843.)

Loudon had firm views on planting, which should evoke a state of quiet repose. A cemetery should not be planted up in the style of a rich man's landscape park, with irregularly scattered clumps of trees and shelter belts. Planting in this way would waste valuable burial space, restrict the free circulation of air and give the cemetery the erroneous character of a park or pleasure ground. Instead, he wished to promote its distinctive character as a place of repose for the dead, and of quiet contemplation for the mourners, who could be expected to return regularly over the months and years. He stipulated 'no flowers at all', as he disliked any ground that 'had the appearance of being dug or moved for the purpose of cultivation'. Trees and shrubs were a key feature but should not 'impede the free circulation of the air and the drying effect of the sun'.

Lines of trees along paths and boundaries would make the most economical use of the grave space available. Individual special specimen trees would indicate junctions and features of particular note. For practical purposes, he recommended trees with narrow conical shapes, such as cypresses, rather than those with 'bulky heads'; he also favoured those that were evergreen and had dark foliage, such as pines, firs, junipers and yews, preferably those varieties that could easily be clipped into columnar forms so that they did not overhang and obstruct grave plots. Dark green, weeping and fastigiate trees were also symbolically appropriate. An exception was made for the trees planted at the intersections of the burial divisions; these could be trees 'of a kind strikingly different from every other planted in the cemetery', to act as markers. The South Metropolitan Cemetery at West Norwood was illustrated in both 'Pleasure Ground' style, with wide spacious lawns leading up to the buildings, clumps and belts of spreading deciduous trees, and concentrations of tombs, and in his contrasting 'Cemetery' style, planted on a more linear pattern with a predominance of fastigiate trees with a pronounced vertical form. His advice became fashionable, evergreens being planted in combination with weeping and fastigiate trees, creating a distinctive funerary style.

For Loudon garden cemeteries were not merely repositories for the

JOHN CLAUDIUS LOUDON

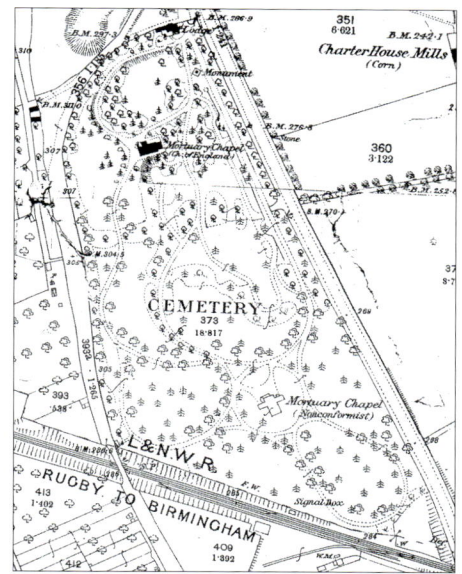

Left: London Road, Coventry, a late privately funded cemetery, was laid out by Joseph Paxton in 1845-7 using the typical components and picturesque serpentine lines in his design. Problems of burial space arose because of the scattered trees and the sharp angles at path junctions.

Above: Monument to the great gardener and engineer Joseph Paxton (1803-65), erected c.1867 in London Road, Coventry. He was also MP for the city.

dead. They were far more than that, being instructive, improving of manners, morals and taste, educational and soothing places for the resort of relatives. The cemetery could be a good reason for visitors to take exercise and fresh air, in the course of a walk out from town, leading to an attachment to it as a place of interment. Indeed, beyond even these multiple functions, a town cemetery 'might become a school of instruction in architecture, sculpture, landscape-gardening, arboriculture, botany and in those important parts of general gardening, neatness, order and high keeping', as well as serving as historical records for local history and biography.

Further cemeteries opened in the 1840s, but still in modest numbers. Loudon contributed to three, at Cambridge (1843), Southampton (partial contribution, 1843) and Abbey Cemetery, Bath (opened 1844). Loudon himself was buried in Kensal Green in 1843. Perhaps the most important cemetery of this decade was London Road, Coventry (1845–7), by the great Joseph Paxton, head gardener at Chatsworth, Derbyshire, who later designed the Crystal Palace for the Great Exhibition in 1851. Part of the site was a former stone quarry, whose hillocks and hollows, surrounded by rows of mature elms, formed one of the main features of the design, with a terrace walk and seats installed in 1849. The cemetery was 'resorted to' by a large number of visitors, and a contemporary account described it as having 'more the air of a gentleman's park than a city of the dead'. Church Cemetery, Nottingham (1848–56), was another sited in a sandstone quarry.

THE GREAT GARDEN OF DEATH, 1850–1901

MOST VICTORIAN CEMETERIES were built in the second half of the century, with a great burst of construction in the 1850s. The second cholera epidemic of 1848–9 prompted government action to improve burial conditions for sanitary purposes, particularly aimed at tightly populated urban areas. In the fifty years between 1859 and 1909 the general population roughly doubled. A series of Acts was passed which became known as the Burial Acts, starting with the London Metropolitan Interments Act in 1850, which were superseded by the Metropolitan Burial Act of 1852. Several more Acts were passed and the Acts were then consolidated in 1857, providing the answer to the burial crisis of the 1830s and 1840s, and allowing a national system of public cemeteries to be established. The time was certainly ripe, for of more than 160 open architectural competitions for cemeteries held between 1843 and 1900 nearly a hundred occurred in the 1850s. The old joint-stock companies that had dominated the earlier cemetery provision continued to run their cemeteries, but nearly all those constructed from the 1850s, with a few notable exceptions, were run by newly constituted public burial boards. Late commercial ventures included Brookwood Cemetery, near Woking, Surrey (1854), Bradford Undercliffe (1854) and the Great Northern Cemetery in London (1861).

Burial boards were appointed by parish vestries and were responsible for providing for the interment of the dead of the parish, which they could do by building a cemetery funded by the Poor Rate. Part could be consecrated, but there had to be an unconsecrated area for Nonconformists. These divisions were marked in various ways. The board was responsible for managing the cemetery, for fixing fees and charges and for the sale of grave plots. Towns and cities took great civic pride in their municipal cemeteries and continued to lay out their new cemetery sites following the pattern of building established since the 1820s. Public cemeteries were provided by burial boards until local government reforms late in the century, when the Local Government Acts of 1894 and 1899 made cemeteries the responsibility of the newly formed local authorities at metropolitan borough, district, town and parish level.

Opposite:
A *porte-cochère*, or covered carriage entrance, surmounted by a belfry, gave shelter to coffins and mourners at the chapel. This is Birkenhead Cemetery (now known as Flaybrick Memorial Gardens), Merseyside.

THE VICTORIAN CEMETERY

Brookwood Cemetery near Woking, the great London cemetery in the Surrey countryside, was opened in 1854. It was established by the London Necropolis and National Mausoleum Company as one of the last privately run cemeteries. This is the Anglican chapel by Sidney Smirke, built in the 1850s.

Widespread creation of cemeteries occurred in a great rush in 1850s and 1860s, based on the garden cemetery model. Most were designed by local or nationally notable architects, by the city or town surveyor or by a landscape designer, or by a combination of these. Sometimes a local architect laid out the site but a more prestigious architect was called upon to design the buildings. This boom was also reflected in the Empire, Europe and North America.

The landscape designer William Gay specialised in cemetery design. As Clerk of Works at Leicester General (1849) and the cemetery's first Superintendent, he laid out several cemeteries, as well as public parks. These included Undercliffe, in Bradford (established 1854), Toxteth Park in Liverpool (opened 1856, the first publicly funded cemetery in Liverpool), and Lawnswood and Pudsey in Leeds (both opened in 1875), for the last of which he designed the buildings. He also designed and laid out others at Bacup, Wigan and Lancaster. Undercliffe was built on 26 acres of farmland costing £3,400, with £12,000 to be spent on laying out the site. A freehold

Left: The division between Anglican and Nonconformist or Dissenters' sections was usually marked. This post was one of a number marking the line between the Dissenters' and Anglican sections at Beckett Street Cemetery, Leeds, opened in 1845.

Right: Plots were marked to aid identification of various areas within the cemetery, which might otherwise be difficult to find. Ceramic grave markers were used at Poole Cemetery, Dorset.

THE GREAT GARDEN OF DEATH, 1850–1901

Italy boasts some of the grandest cemeteries of the Victorian period. Cimitero Monumentale, Milan, opened in 1866. It has an extraordinary collection of sculpture and monuments, including temples, obelisks and even a scaled-down version of the antique Roman Trajan's Column.

grave in the most prestigious part of the cemetery cost 10 guineas (£10.50), with rates decreasing proportionately to one guinea for an average grave. Edward Kemp, a prolific designer who worked for Joseph Paxton and was Superintendent at Birkenhead Park, laid out the City of Liverpool Cemetery, Anfield (opened 1863), and Birkenhead Cemetery (opened 1864, now known as Flaybrick Memorial Gardens) to very attractive designs, and he advised on planting at St Helens.

Loudon's preferred grid plan quickly superseded serpentine layouts. Some exceptions occurred, such as Gay's Lawnswood, Leeds, and Stoke-on-Trent

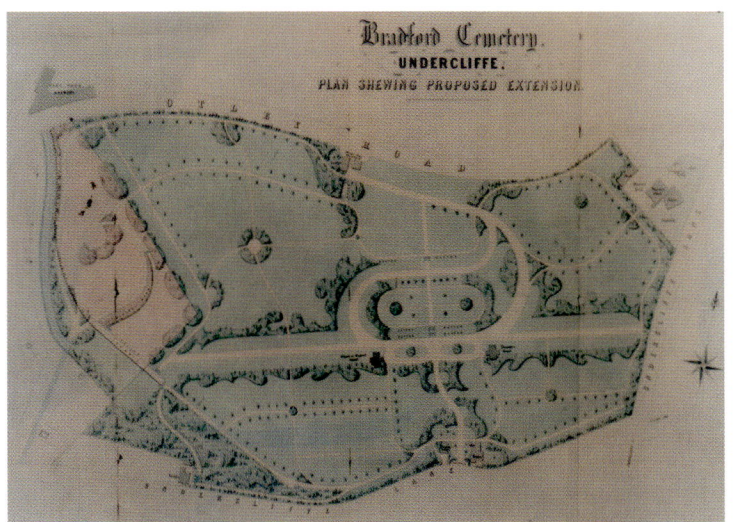

Undercliffe Cemetery, Bradford, opened in 1854, was another late privately run cemetery. The design by William Gay captured panoramic views from the main promenade. Gay's layout was amended in 1876 to show a proposed western extension, which was never achieved, leaving Gay very embittered.

33

by H. E. Milner (*c.* 1884), but the grid made most efficient use of space, often with a central single chapel complex, such as at Bridlington, East Yorkshire (1880), perhaps supplemented by circular paths or carriage sweeps as part of the geometric pattern.

Throughout Britain, cities established one or usually more large cemeteries, as at Liverpool, Birmingham and Manchester. London's 'Magnificent Seven' cemeteries were by now established and successful, but further provision was required as London continued to expand. Notable cemeteries were established by St Pancras and Islington parishes in East Finchley (1854, the first burial board cemetery in London), by the City of Westminster at Hanwell (1854), by the City of London at Little Ilford (1856), the Great Northern Cemetery by a company at Colney Hatch (1861–3), by the local burial board at Hampstead (1874–6), and by Wandsworth Borough Council at Putney Vale (1891).

Jewish cemeteries were laid out in London and beyond, including one at Buckingham Road, West Ham (1857; 10 acres). This has a magnificent mausoleum to Evelina de Rothschild (1866), commissioned by her heartbroken husband, Ferdinand, from the architect Matthew Digby Wyatt. Willesden Jewish Cemetery (1873; 23 acres), designed by Nathan Joseph, is regarded as the most prestigious among London's Jewish cemeteries. Plymouth Jewish Cemetery is a typical modest provincial example, which replaced a mid-eighteenth-century one on Plymouth Hoe in the 1860s. It had a conventional grid system, with a lodge and gateway, and was surrounded by high walls, next to the main Plymouth Cemetery.

One of the most imposing and most influential of the early public cemeteries was the City of London, at Little Ilford, then on the edge of the capital's suburbs, with its combination of formal and picturesque elements. An angled carriage drive formed the spinal axis, off which led grand formal

Plymouth Jewish Cemetery dates from the 1860s.

THE GREAT GARDEN OF DEATH, 1850–1901

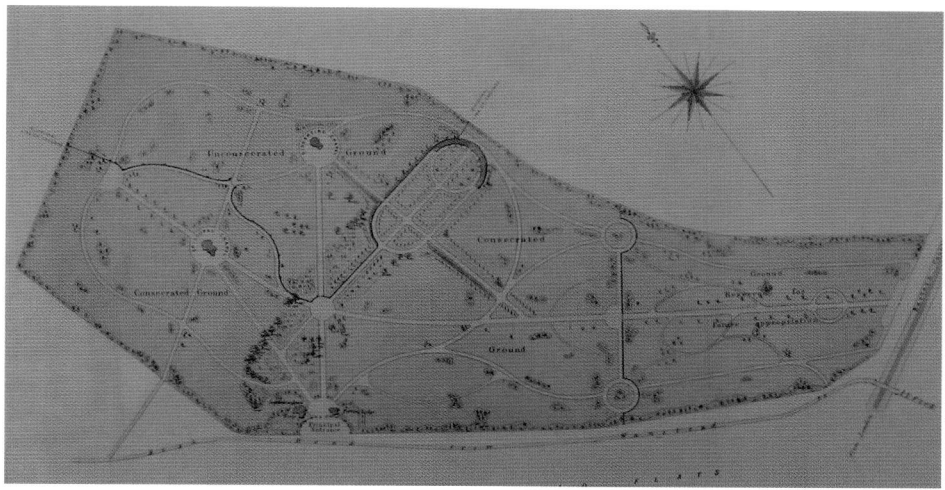

One of the great publicly run cemeteries was the City of London Cemetery, Little Ilford, Essex. The 80-acre site was 7 miles from the centre of London. It included a great gateway, superintendent's house, catacombs and Dissenters' and Anglican chapels. (Plan by William Haywood, 1856.)

features, including the wide main drives, the carriage turns about the chapels and the sunken oval of the catacombs, set within a less formal landscape of long, curving paths and scattered trees, planted both singly and in groups. It was laid out on an 80-acre site and landscaped by Robert Davidson with architect William Haywood at a cost of £45,450. In 1858 2,681 interments took place, with over half a million since.

The largest cemetery in Europe was and remains Brookwood in Surrey – London's vast country cemetery, unique in various respects. It was one of the last to be founded by a commercial company, when burial board and municipal cemeteries became the norm, and in this respect was an oddity. Even so, it epitomised the Victorian garden cemetery and was a phenomenon. Brookwood was founded in 1852 by the London Necropolis and National Mausoleum Company (LNC) to house London's dead forever. An Act of Parliament allowed the company to purchase 2,268 acres of heathland near Woking from Lord Onslow for £35,000 to provide a cemetery. A cemetery of that size was not envisaged, but the establishment of the cemetery allowed the company to acquire a large area of land at reduced cost for speculative building. Work began

The Anglican chapel by William Haywood at the City of London Cemetery. He also designed the Dissenters' chapel, catacombs, entrance gates and lodges. (*The Builder*, December 1855.)

THE VICTORIAN CEMETERY

The City of London Cemetery, laid out in 1853–6, had a magnificent group of buildings and overall design by William Haywood. The landscaping was by the London landscape gardener Robert Davidson. These views show the main gateway and lodges, and the catacombs.

immediately on 350 acres at Brookwood, serviced by its own railway line, planted to J. C. Loudon's principles and enclosed by an 8-foot high wall. In 1854 'Mr Thomas, the Landscape Gardener, had been engaged to prepare a plan for the ornamental laying out and planting of the cemetery' for £32 0s. 0d. This was presumably the prestigious landscaper William Broderick Thomas, who later designed the gardens of Sandringham House for the Prince of Wales. The chapels and stations were designed by Sidney Smirke, and the landscaping and extensive evergreen planting were carried out over several years by the local nurseryman Robert Donald, whose father had been an associate of Loudon.

Division into two large Anglican and Nonconformist sections was achieved at Brookwood using a long, straight, walled public road. By 1900 four main chapels were provided, two Anglican, one Nonconformist and one Roman Catholic. The Anglican section was consecrated in the Anglican chapel in a ceremony conducted as usual by the local bishop, in this case the Bishop of Winchester, in November 1854. A special train brought shareholders and directors of the LNC and directors of the London & South Western Railway. After the service the grounds were viewed and a light lunch was served in the station before the return train to London.

Undercliff Cemetery, Bradford, was consecrated in August 1854 by the Bishop of Ripon at a ceremony attended by more than four thousand people. A procession led from the lodge to the chapel, where Divine Service was held. It was a grand civic event as well as a religious one, attended by the Mayor, the Town Clerk and members of the town council, directors and shareholders, and various clergy and choristers.

Various denominations and London parishes had their own dedicated plots enclosed at Brookwood, including the Parsee burial ground, unique in England, together with various guilds and organisations such as the Oddfellows' Society, the Ancient Order of Foresters and the London & South Western Railway. Brochures were regularly produced describing the foundation of the London Necropolis, the conduct of funerals, the burial site and scales of charges, with quotations from newspapers and journals testifying to the sanitary and other advantages of burial there.

Other types of cemeteries appeared, usually to serve specific institutions where considerable numbers of deaths occurred, particularly hospitals, asylums, prisons and military garrisons. These followed the established pattern, combining ornament with utility. The Royal Victoria Military Hospital at Netley near Southampton was constructed alongside Southampton Water in the mid 1850s after the Crimean War and opened in 1863 with an attractive dedicated cemetery within the extensive grounds. The cemetery lay remote from the main building, out of sight some half a mile away; although on a grid pattern, it occupied a gentle slope within woodland and was clothed with conifers and evergreens and acquired many headstones. The mid-nineteenth-century garrison at Aldershot was served by its own cemetery, laid out by the Royal Engineers in 1853–4 as part of the military camp. It was enclosed by iron railings and managed by the military authorities – from the 1870s by the Royal Engineers. In 1879 the original wooden mortuary chapel was replaced by one of brick. Serpentine drives and paths gently flowed down the slopes ornamented with a wide variety of mature trees and shrubs, with many evergreens, including wellingtonias and cedars. Banks of evergreen laurel, rhododendron and clipped yews defined the various areas. Much effort and pride were expended on these institutional cemeteries. Some lunatic asylums had their own cemeteries, which were usually more utilitarian in their design and planting and seldom had headstones as they served only pauper patients. Examples included Warlingham in Surrey, High Royds at Menston in West Yorkshire and Leavesden in Hertfordshire.

Even the new cemeteries began to fill up as the population grew

A traditional country lychgate was erected by the parish of St Alban's, Holborn, at the entrance to their enclosure at Brookwood, a plot allocated for a specific London congregation. It was one of four lychgates in the cemetery.

THE VICTORIAN CEMETERY

inexorably. Those within urban areas could not be extended, but many had been sited on the urban fringes, and where development had not engulfed them there was space for them to be extended. Often efforts were made to ensure that the design of the new section fitted with the old, for example at Stapenhill, Burton upon Trent. Here the original 12 acres was enlarged to 22 acres in 1883, the new ground being laid out in a similar style to the existing area, with a central avenue and circular walks. Cemeteries continued to be opened on new sites throughout the century.

CHAPELS

The chapel or chapels formed the focus of the cemetery design and of the religious ceremony before the interment. They were generally in some kind of Gothic style, with one or more lodges in a similar style or perhaps

A grand ensemble of chapels was common. Here a pair of parallel stone chapels is linked by a *porte-cochère* with a dramatic spire at Bridlington Cemetery, East Yorkshire (c. 1880), by the architect Alfred Smith of Nottingham.

Trowbridge Cemetery, Wiltshire, is a good example of the numerous burial board cemeteries of the 1850s. The separate chapels, set within their own sections, were designed by Charles Davies of Bath in 1854. Unusually, the Nonconformist chapel (left) is more elaborate than the Anglican one (right).

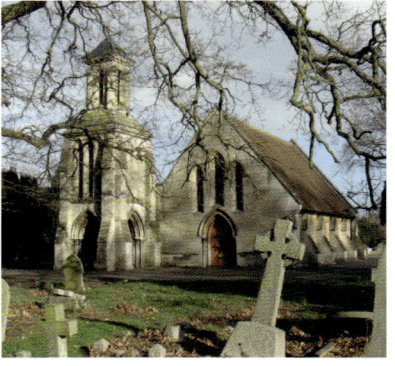

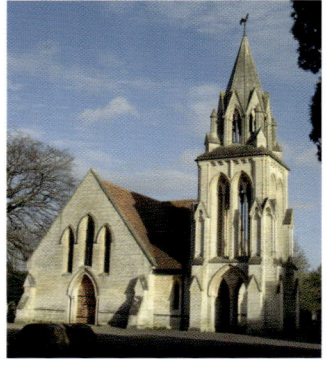

38

THE GREAT GARDEN OF DEATH, 1850–1901

Jacobethan. A number of architectural firms specialised in cemeteries, particularly in the 1850s and 1860s, for example the London partnership of John Barnett and W. C. Birch, and the Cheltenham architect W. H. Knight, who designed cemeteries at Cheltenham (1861–2), Hereford (1858), Great Malvern (1861) and Shipston-on-Stour (1863). The Liverpool architect T. D. Barry designed the buildings of Toxteth Park Cemetery (1855) and Liverpool Cemetery (c.1860, with layout by Edward Kemp), and many of the burial board cemeteries in south Lancashire.

Most of the larger cemeteries were furnished with two chapels, for Anglicans and Nonconformists, although the smaller town cemeteries such as Tunbridge Wells had only one. Sometimes a third chapel was provided for

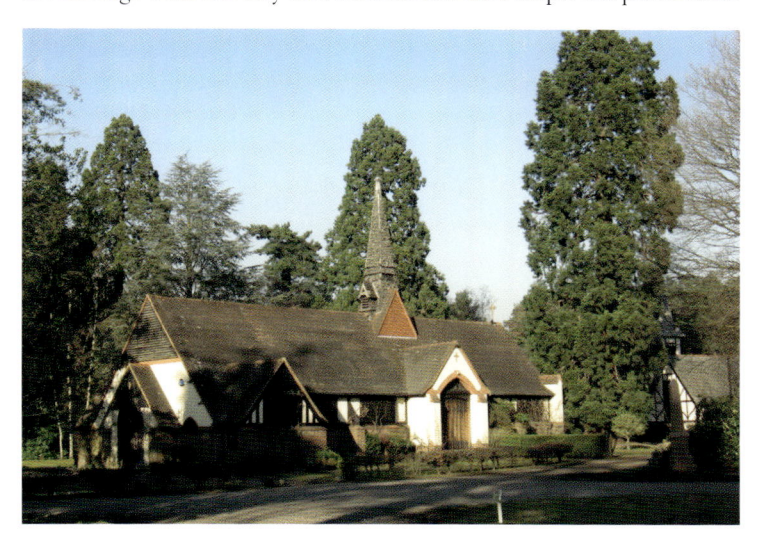

Above left: Gothic chapels at Horsforth Cemetery, Leeds, illustrated in *The Builder*, 1881. They were built at right angles to each other and divided by the tall tower. This was a typical arrangement of chapels.

Above right: The lodge at Highgate (1837) proudly announced the Elysium beyond as a magnificent gateway to heaven. (*The Mirror*, September 1838.)

The Anglican chapels at Brookwood Cemetery, Surrey, were unusually not built of stone but timber-framed and rendered. This is the second one (1908–10) is by Tubbs & Messer in similar style to Smirke's earlier one of 1854.

THE VICTORIAN CEMETERY

Lodges stood at the gates and housed the superintendent and office: (top) Utley, West Yorkshire; (middle left) Harrogate, North Yorkshire, 1864; (middle right) Trowbridge, Wiltshire, by Charles Davies, 1854.

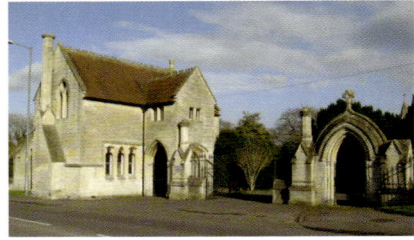

Most town cemeteries had one or more lodges at the gateway. The lodge at the entrance to Bridlington Cemetery is in flamboyant Victorian Gothic style with polychrome brickwork and elegant iron roof finials, by Alfred Smith of Nottingham, c.1880. Its vivid colouring is complemented by the bright seasonal bedding, an echo of the late-Victorian scheme.

40

Roman Catholics, such as at City Road, Sheffield, and Ulverston, Cumbria. The two main chapels were often presented as a single composite building, with the buildings set parallel or at right angles to each other, often linked by a *porte-cochère*, or covered carriage entrance, and topped by a tower or spire. This created an imposing focus to the whole cemetery, for example at Bridlington (by Alfred Smith of Nottingham, *c.*1880), and Bouncers Lane, Cheltenham (W. H. Knight, mid 1860s). Barnsley Cemetery had a great open screen linking the two imposing parallel chapels of 1860 by Perkin and Backhouse. Elsewhere separate chapels stood within their own denominational section, for example at Trowbridge, Wiltshire, and Poole, Dorset (both 1854).

MONUMENTS

Monuments accumulated across the cemetery over the decades and defined it as a place for the dead, as well as identifying their social standing within the collection. The grave plots could be bought in perpetuity and so the monuments were left permanently in position to commemorate individuals or families. They were made for a wide range of people, whose social and financial status they reflected in their size and elaboration, and they were generally gravestones, tombs or mausolea.

Social standing was reflected in the position of plots within the cemetery, often with a differential pricing in particular areas so that the most impressive monuments were grouped together on the most prestigious and expensive plots. This is especially evident at Undercliffe, Bradford (William Gay, 1852–4). Here the great spinal terrace, formerly focused on the chapel (now demolished), contains rows of the most impressive monuments and mausolea, packed together on either side of the broad sweep like a town. Conversely, at Trowbridge, Wiltshire, the three mausolea are sited far both from each other and from the central axial drive, and ranged around the perimeter of the cemetery.

Public graves for paupers were provided in most cemeteries. The plots were communal, taking many bodies, and generally unmarked except for ephemeral wooden markers. These plots appear now as uncharacteristically open areas of grass in cemeteries crowded with monuments elsewhere, but they may contain the remains of many people, as at Beckett Street, Leeds. Brookwood has extensive areas of unmarked pauper burials from London parishes.

Guinea graves were a solution to the shame of an unmarked pauper's grave. A single plot was used for many unrelated people; for example, in Beckett Street, Leeds, the bodies of thirty-eight adults, children and babies were buried in just over a month in one grave opened in 1856. One guinea (£1.05, or around a week's wages for many of the population) purchased a place in the plot

THE VICTORIAN CEMETERY

A group of 'guinea graves' in the Dissenters' section at Beckett Street, Leeds. The headstones reflect the number of unrelated people buried in each plot, and names are often inscribed on both sides of the slabs. A place in such a grave cost one guinea (£1.05).

and up to thirty-six letters of inscription on a communal headstone. Beckett Street has an unusually large number of these memorials, mostly dating from the 1870s to the 1930s – nearly identical, large plain headstones inscribed on both sides with a long list of unrelated names.

Grave plots were marked by a variety of headstones, the simplest being single vertical slabs, some with kerbs marking out the plot in front, or with footstones at the far end of the plot. Some plots were enclosed by railings on a kerb or by bollards with iron chains. Relief sculpture on the slab could be of a very high standard and depicted themes such as stylised flowers and

Slab memorials in Exeter Higher Cemetery: (left) Bombardier Scattergood died heroically in the Exeter theatre fire in 1887 and his friends erected this monument; (middle) a bronze plaque in Art Nouveau style was attached to a stone monolith to commemorate William Prowse, the Assistant City Surveyor of Exeter, who died in 1898, aged thirty-six; (right) a fine relief sculpture of a rose, perhaps depicting Agnes Eliza Toms.

THE GREAT GARDEN OF DEATH, 1850–1901

Above:
The deceased's profession was sometimes represented on the monument, for example these anchors for seafarers in Knaresborough (right) and Harrogate (left). The anchor also symbolised hope and a firm faith in salvation. Freemasons often used a fouled anchor with a piece of rope entwined, as in the right-hand monument.

Left:
The professional and family association of Thomas Longman of the publishing firm was commemorated with a stone book (1879) in Poole, Dorset. This might also represent the testament, the Book of Life.

43

THE VICTORIAN CEMETERY

Particular events might be represented. Sergeant-Major Johnston was one of the few men to survive the Charge of the Light Brigade in the Crimea in 1854, when he was aged twenty-one. He died in 1882, aged forty-nine, a veteran of many more campaigns. This monument is in Harrogate, North Yorkshire.

vegetation, particularly such blooms as lilies and passion-flowers, which had particular meaning in the language of death.

More elaborate monuments were erected by wealthier families, who commissioned a great variety of sculpture with a wide range of themes. Some were symbolic of death, such as obelisks, broken columns and draped crosses; others represented allegorical figures such as angels and cherubs, or the

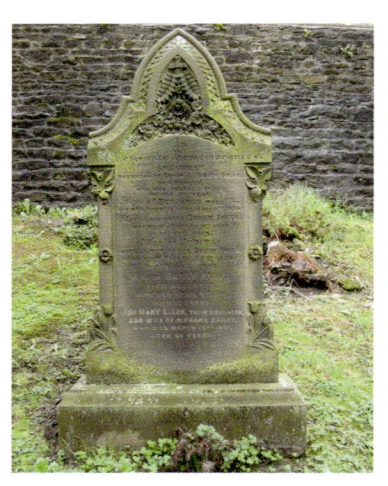

High-quality carving was often executed on even modest stones, and flowers and foliage were common subjects because of their aesthetic qualities and symbolism. (Left) The memorial to Susannah Smith, who died in 1858, and her brother Benjamin, who died in 1868, both aged two, is in Utley, West Yorkshire. (Right) The lily symbolised chastity, innocence or purity; this monument is in Brookwood, Surrey.

THE GREAT GARDEN OF DEATH, 1850–1901

Above: There was a tradition of cemeteries in country-house gardens for family pets or even favourite horses, but by the end of the nineteenth century urban pets had their own public cemeteries, such as at Hyde Park.

Right: Wilson's Monument in Ulverston Cemetery, Cumbria, is a marble scale replica of a lighthouse, with carved rocks and waves around the base. It commemorates Thomas Watkins Wilson MD, who died in 1897. The tapered shaft is incised to represent ashlar blocks, a doorway and window openings. A glass lantern originally enclosed a gas jet. The base is carved with an anchor and chain. The lighthouse could also represent the beacon for the soul: 'I am the light of the world' (John 8:12).

deceased and his or her mourning family. The unusual memorial to Sarah Norwood (died 1851) in Abney Park Cemetery shows a draped beehive without bees in evidence. Monuments sometimes reflected the occupation of the deceased; anchors, for example, were commonly used for seafaring men, although they also symbolised hope.

Mausolea were commissioned by the wealthiest families to house the remains of several generations. These structures became more common in the eighteenth and early nineteenth centuries for aristocratic families on their country estates. They were further popularised by the construction of two royal mausolea in the grounds of Frogmore House at Windsor, for the Duchess of Kent, and for Queen Victoria and Prince Albert, completed in the 1860s. In cemeteries they were a particular phenomenon of the mid to late nineteenth century. Freestanding buildings, which could be almost as large as the cemetery chapels, they took a variety of shapes and sizes and might be designed by prestigious architects. They usually had an iron gate or wooden or metal door, and shelves inside to hold the coffins. Sometimes the coffins

THE VICTORIAN CEMETERY

Mausolea were designed in many different styles, and an Egyptian style was used by the Illingworth family at Undercliffe, Bradford. Strictly, it is a 'mastaba' – an underground room for burial with an area above in which to place offerings, in this case the urns containing the ashes of family members.

The Nicols family mausoleum (c.1897), a Gothic private chapel in the Roman Catholic section at Brookwood, Surrey.

Below:
Two mausolea in Brookwood: (Below left) the Keith family mausoleum (c.1890); (Below right) the columbarium originally constructed for Lord Cadogan in c.1878–80.

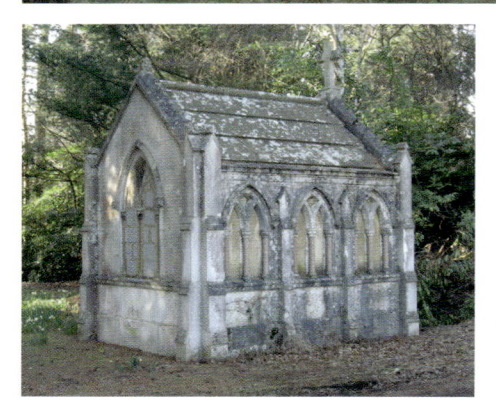

THE GREAT GARDEN OF DEATH, 1850–1901

Above: This grand mausoleum, c.1875, with a miniature chapel above, is in a modest cemetery at Utley, West Yorkshire. The Butterfield family chapel and vault face the main gateway. The vault is set into a bank.

Right: Some mausolea were of more exotic form, such as this one in Mortlake Roman Catholic Cemetery, London. Built of rendered stone and resembling an Arab tent, it was designed for Sir Richard Burton, who died in Trieste in 1890, by his wife Isabel, who is also buried there.

Below: Other denominations sometimes had grounds within a larger cemetery. The Parsee or Zoroastrian cemetery at Brookwood, Surrey, was begun in 1862. The two obelisks mark the original entrance and frame the tomb of Nowrosjee Nusserwanji Wadia, who died in 1899.

THE VICTORIAN CEMETERY

Above: Even within cemeteries, which were enclosed by walls or railings and locked at night, iron railings were used around monuments. The Rosary in Norwich has several elegant patterns.

Left: At Harrogate, unusually muscular iron bollards enclose two plots.

Below left: Ironwork was used for various purposes. These gates mark the bridge crossing the catacombs ring to give access to the central 'island' at Glasnevin, Dublin.

Below right: An iron gate at Knaresborough, North Yorkshire.

48

THE GREAT GARDEN OF DEATH, 1850–1901

were buried below the structure and an altar for prayer was provided above. Queen Victoria's mausoleum is the epitome of this type. No single architectural style was adopted, but a variety of historical styles was used, including Gothic, neo-Greek and Italianate. Egyptian was popular because of its direct association with ancient pyramidal tombs and indirect symbolic reference to freemasonry. A notable group of mausolea stands in the Parsee section of Brookwood Cemetery, dominated by that of Nowrosjee Nusserwanji Wadia (died 1899) at the centre of the area, with a group for the notable Indian Tata family set among pines.

Various materials were used for monuments but most were fashioned from the local stone, such as limestone, slate or sandstone, or from imported marble. There was often a stonemason's yard attached to the cemetery, or it might even occupy part of the grounds, as at Brookwood and York, where it formed part of the commercial operation of the cemetery companies. Italian

Individual burial grounds were set aside within Brookwood, Surrey. They served particular London parishes or non-denominational groups of people such as staff of the London & South Western Railway and members of the Ancient Order of Foresters. Iron entrance pillars were used to mark the entrance to St Anne's Ground, one of the individual London parish plots within the cemetery.

Bottom left: Iron was used for both elaborate and simple memorials. The Hines family memorial in The Rosary, Norwich, is surmounted by a birdbath. The miniature heads fixed to it are reputedly representations of family members. The family ran an ironfounding business in Norwich.

Bottom right: An elegant cast-iron monument to Ann Farrow (died 1854) in West Norwood, London.

THE VICTORIAN CEMETERY

Top left:
This elegant iron cross at Brookwood, Surrey, is unusual. It stands in the prestigious Ring area, said to be the 'Westminster Abbey' of Victorian London's middle class.

Top right:
Sculpture on monuments could be of the highest quality. One of the most important monuments at Brookwood, Surrey, is the bronze memorial to Lady Matilda Jane Pelham-Clinton (died 1892) and Lord Edward Pelham-Clinton (died 1907).

marble was often used for sculptures such as statues and angels and a range of standard designs was imported from Italy already sculpted. Other materials included iron, brick, terracotta, artificial stone such as Coade stone, plaster, bronze, copper and wood. Combinations of these might be used for more elaborate memorials, particularly mausolea, which were generally built of some kind of stone or of brick rendered to resemble stone. At Brookwood

Cast iron was a speciality of New Orleans, Louisiana, and was also used in the city's many high-quality cemeteries. A number of iron mausolea were erected, including the Karstendiek tomb in Lafayette Cemetery No. 1.

THE GREAT GARDEN OF DEATH, 1850–1901

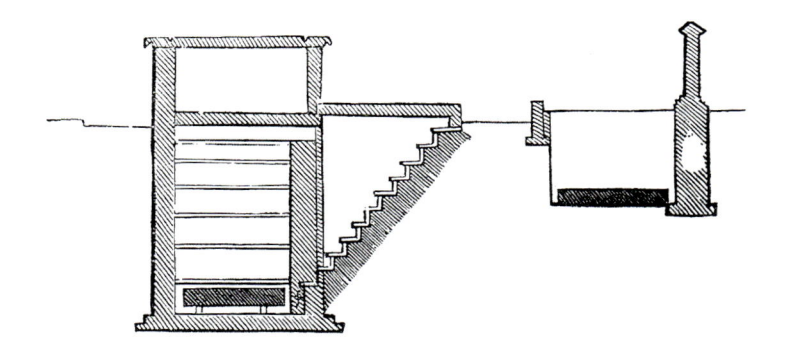

The structure of catacombs is rarely visible as it is mainly below ground. This cross-section (left) shows access via a flight of steps covered by a flagstone. Beside it is an ordinary grave (right), with a headstone and footstone. (J. C. Loudon, On the Laying Out of Cemeteries, 1843.)

the base of the monument to Giulio Salviati (died 1898), a Venetian glass and mosaic merchant, has four high-quality mosaic panels, gilded and coloured, executed by his firm. Each depicts flowers of remembrance and mourning: lilies, forget-me-nots, roses and laurel. Inscriptions could be incised or sit proud of the surface, or be gilded, painted or filled with metal such as lead.

Vaults, although largely unseen, were an essential element of the cemetery for those too poor to afford a mausoleum but who wanted a family plot of some standing and were rich enough to pay for more than an ordinary grave. A vault is a substantial masonry structure within a plot, divided vertically into cells, one for each coffin, with each being sealed by brickwork or a memorial tablet. Loudon illustrated a typical cross-section, with steps leading down to the lowest level of interment, the steps usually covered by a flat stone. Alternatively ordinary graves, commonly 10 to 20 feet deep, were brick-lined and covered with a large flat stone, a ledger stone. The side walls were constructed as arches to support the sides against the pressure of the soil, and ledges were constructed on which the coffin would be placed, or else it was raised above the one below by slate slabs or iron bars.

Burial receipt for a freehold brick grave lined to take five burials at Undercliffe, Bradford, and including the first interment, that of George Scholey, in May 1865 at a cost of £4 9s. 6d.

PLANTING

Loudon's planting was intended to evoke mourning and contemplation, but he also recommended botanical diversity, which remained popular in the later nineteenth century. The trees were the most important planting in the Victorian cemetery, providing long-term structure and clothing otherwise stark lines. Evergreens were usually the mainstay, such as the ubiquitous yew, and also holly, holm-oak, wellingtonia and cedars, but deciduous species such as oak, beech and plane were also planted. The Wellingtonia was not introduced until 1853 (the year of the Iron Duke's death) and with its fastigiate

Planting often followed Loudon's guidance, for example here at Brookwood Cemetery, Surrey, with many fastigiate conifers (right). Magnificent avenues of nineteenth-century Wellingtonias dominate both Anglican (below) and unconsecrated (below right) sections, possibly the best collection in England.

THE GREAT GARDEN OF DEATH, 1850–1901

Postcards of the cemetery announced the last resting place of the deceased. At Brockley, south London, these large planting displays embellished the avenue to the chapel.

By the late nineteenth century gay floral displays were used along the main public routes (although Loudon would have disapproved) in the same way as in public parks. This bedding display is along the main avenue leading to the chapels at Ryde, Isle of Wight.

habit was ideal for cemeteries, although it became very broad at the base in maturity if grown well. The planting at Brookwood reflected Loudon's idea of 'appropriate' planting for cemeteries, including extensive use of dark-foliaged evergreens, weeping and fastigiate trees, and a move away from the flower beds and 'pleasure-ground' type of planting seen in some earlier public cemeteries. The site was planted with a huge number of trees, including striking avenues of great monkey-puzzles, and a wide variety of other conifers. Several monumental avenues of wellingtonia were planted there and form one of the earliest and most extensive collections of the species in Britain.

Later in the century more colour was used, including flowering trees and shrubs such as rhododendrons, but also

Graves were ornamented by loved ones with flowers, either real or artificial. This ceramic floral grave decoration at Plymouth Road, Tavistock, Devon, is covered by a glass dome, similar to nineteenth-century examples.

53

THE VICTORIAN CEMETERY

Even elaborate carpet-bedding schemes were used, such as were commonly found in public parks. Bishopwearmouth, Sunderland.

bedding of similar type to that used extensively in public parks. Loudon had expressly avoided this. The lawn in front of the main gate at Bridlington is still brightly bedded out, complementing the polychrome brickwork of the lodge. In 1890 the landscape designer Henry Milner recommended planting of mixed evergreens and deciduous shrubs, mainly of flowering types with bright blossoms and on raised mounds. An avenue of alternate monkey-puzzles and clipped golden holly still lines the main drive to the chapel at Wimborne Road, Bournemouth (opened 1878). Cedars encircled the chapels at Brandwood End, Birmingham (opened 1898); cypresses and variegated evergreens lined the main drive, with copper beeches and an avenue of wellingtonia for the cross paths. Hendon (founded 1899), in north-west London, was one of the last Victorian cemeteries. It was crossed by a stream with several rustic bridges and, according to the 1903 brochure, planted with thousands of trees and shrubs, including, around the cemetery boundary, 'a row of evergreen firs, pine, ilexes and hollies and another row of black poplars alternating with oaks, elms, maples, ashes and other deciduous trees'. A host of flowers and creepers disguised every wall and waste heap.

At Wimborne Road, Bournemouth, an unusual avenue of monkey-puzzles and golden hollies was planted along the main drive to the chapel. The whole cemetery was enclosed and protected from maritime storms by a belt of trees, including pines and hollies.

RAILWAYS

Cemeteries were designed with paths and drives for use by pedestrians and horse-drawn carriages and hearses. Although railways were embraced by Victorian society and industry wholeheartedly throughout the kingdom, surprisingly railway travel for funerals and mourners to cemeteries never became popular. At Brookwood, however, these two great phenomena of the Victorian age, the railway and the cemetery, were inextricably and successfully united, but this was a rare occurrence, unique in Britain. However, because it was so successful a part of this cemetery's working for over eighty years, it deserves further discussion.

Apart from Brookwood Cemetery's size, its most distinctive feature was the branch line off the main London & South Western Railway, linking the two halves of the cemetery. The cemetery was served by a purpose-built and dedicated receiving station at Waterloo, 25 miles away, essential to convey both mourners and coffins from the London catchment area. The journey to Woking was said to pass 'comforting scenery' for the mourners. Special tickets were issued for mourners and corpses using the Necropolis train, in the standard three classes for both: first, second and third. The maximum charge to convey mourners and attendants was set in the LNC's 1852 Act at 6s. 0d for first class, 3s. 6d for second class, and 2s. 0d for third class. The charges for bodies were: pauper 2s. 6d, artisan 5s. 0d, and all others £1. Mourners' tickets were always issued as returns, while the tickets for coffins were issued only as singles. Special hearse vans were constructed for the LNC

The southern section of the Brookwood Railway with the first Anglican chapel by Sidney Smirke (1850s) and a station.

THE VICTORIAN CEMETERY

The Brookwood Cemetery Railway. (Above left) The nouthern section of the railway, showing a station and platform. (Above right) A cemetery train, showing the track lined by low hedges and flanked by a Wellingtonia avenue.

with different compartments for the three coffin classes, while mourners travelled on the same train as the deceased in standard passenger carriages. Segregation of coffins by religious denomination was notionally also practised but not always strictly adhered to. Within the cemetery were two stations, one for each section, each with its own platform, refreshment and waiting rooms, near the three main chapels. The refreshment room was not restricted to non-alcoholic drinks, as a stock book exists of the receipt of spirits for sale at the North Bar, North Station, covering the period 1854–1923. The service ran for over eighty years, until the Waterloo receiving station was largely demolished by a bomb during the Second World War.

The LNC pioneered railway funerals, but many other cemeteries lay next to railway lines and some used the railway to receive funeral parties. No other cemetery in Britain succeeded in providing a dedicated line leading through the cemetery as was done at Brookwood, which seems to have offered a model to the Birmingham Burial Board in the late 1850s. The Birmingham Board hoped to construct a cemetery to serve their metropolis well outside the city at Knowle, served by trains in a similar manner, but the corporation rejected the board's proposals, whereupon its members met and resigned *en masse*. A railway siding and special station had been envisaged for the City of London Cemetery at Little Ilford, but this was never constructed because it was too expensive for the London parishes to wish to fund.

The Great Northern Cemetery at Colney Hatch, London, had a private station at the edge of the cemetery, with trains run by the Great Northern Railway from King's Cross, but this was used only in the 1860s. *The Builder* in 1861 and 1862 described details of the fifteen-minute rail journey, including the hydraulic lift that lowered the coffin in the receiving station to the level of the railway platform. Several cemeteries in Australia were served by rail, the most notable being Rookwood, Sydney (at 777 acres the largest cemetery in the world), opened in 1867, whose railway system was closely based on that of the LNC. It had an elaborate receiving station built of sandstone in Sydney.

PEOPLE

A dedicated hierarchy of staff was headed by the Superintendent (Loudon's 'curator'), who was often a horticulturist and had a staff of gardeners to tend the grounds. Brookwood also had two gatekeepers and eighteen porters. By 1872 York Cemetery was headed by a gardener/superintendent, Stephen Ansell, whose salary was £100 per annum. When he left that year, sixty-six candidates applied for the job. His replacement, Thomas Brown of Boston, served for thirty-seven years and continued until he was over eighty years old, having built up a flourishing stonemasonry business for the company. His success was rewarded by the shareholders and he ended with a salary of £160 per annum. Burial services were generally conducted by a chaplain who was also the incumbent of a local parish or chapel. The Reverend George Henry Hewison, rector of St Dennis Walmgate, York, and York Cemetery chaplain from 1877, was paid £100 per annum and was also chaplain of York Union Workhouse.

CREMATION

Cremation gained credence during the later nineteenth century throughout Europe as an efficient and effective way to dispose of bodies, and the Cremation Society of England was formed in 1874. There was, opposition from orthodox Christians, who objected to burning bodies, but radicals embraced the idea. The first significant crematorium was erected at Woking in 1889. Several others followed in the 1890s, including Manchester (1892), Glasgow (1895) and Liverpool (1896). The most spectacular, however, was Golders Green, London (1902), with a complex of red-brick chapels, arcaded cloisters, columbarium and towers designed by Sir Ernest George and Alfred B. Yeates. The renowned gardener William Robinson advised on the landscaping, being a director of the company and an enthusiast for the process. It was designed to be within easy driving distance of central London and rapidly became the most important crematorium in England. It was set in 12 acres of landscaped gardens, which were not used for burials but designed to be an informal and contemplative setting for funerals. The main memorials are two mausolea and a few statues, but most memorials were plaques and commemorative tablets placed on the boundary and cloister walls, in the columbaria, or adjacent to specific plants. The second crematorium in London was built shortly afterwards at the City of London Cemetery by D. J. Ross, who provided it with two coke-fired furnaces and an 80-foot high chimney within a Gothic building.

PARADISE PRESERVED? THE CEMETERIES TODAY

THE death of the Queen-Empress Victoria in January 1901 effectively concluded the era. She herself was carried much of the way to her grave by railway and was interred in a burial ground not attached to a place of worship, although her mausoleum was a private chapel. Fewer new cemeteries were built in the later part of her reign. Many of the earlier ones were extended once or more, with the extensions often in a different, more utilitarian style, and these extensions continued into the twentieth century. After the First World War many cemeteries had an area laid out for war graves, which are now maintained by the Commonwealth War Graves Commission. Crematoria were sometimes constructed in new buildings in cemeteries or in adapted chapels and memorial gardens, and columbariums were built to house ashes. Some privately run cemeteries were taken over by local authorities, so that only a few remained in private ownership, such as Kensal Green.

Cemetery records survive in various places. Minute books recording the creation of the cemetery are often lodged in county or district archives, together with layout and plot plans, but may still remain with the local authority or cemetery company, or even at the cemetery office itself. The cemetery may still use the earliest plot plan as a working guide to locate graves.

The cult of death declined in the twentieth century, together with the popularity of the cemetery as a prestigious amenity to visit deceased loved ones and for quiet recreation. In the later twentieth century the prestige of Victorian cemeteries declined alarmingly; they were sometimes badly neglected, or their monuments, particularly the kerbs, were removed to simplify maintenance. This was especially damaging as the monuments and their unique arrangement of designs and their grouping defined the cemetery character within the landscape design.

Loudon had envisaged that cemeteries would fill. He believed that, when full, they should be closed as burial grounds and re-opened as public walks or gardens, retaining all monuments at public expense. Instead, in the twentieth century cemeteries that became full, and thus unable to generate an income from burials, were not transformed into public amenities in perpetuity and were often vulnerable to neglect. Buildings and monuments collapsed or became dangerous, and scrub and trees grew between monuments and where there should have been lawn. Often neglect and unchecked vegetation have been justified on grounds of their value for nature conservation. While this is often a significant aspect of the cemetery, it should not be used as an excuse for minimising maintenance, and the historic design and features should not be allowed to become damaged. This eventuality is particularly evident where cemeteries were owned privately, for example at Arnos Vale in Bristol, Undercliffe in Bradford, and in London at Nunhead and Highgate. Local authorities in some cases also neglected their cemeteries or even did their best to destroy them. Notoriously, and possibly at the nadir of the Victorian cemetery, in 1986 Westminster Council sold three major burial board cemeteries (Paddington, St Marylebone and Westminster) for 15p each to save maintenance and management costs. The developers who bought them failed to maintain them to the standards demanded by the relatives of those interred; the council was forced to regain possession of them and restore them to good condition.

Some cemeteries declined into a state of devastation but, like the 'Westminster Three', have had a renaissance, due largely to dedicated local residents who have formed into Friends groups as a force for restoration and re-use. In 1976 Bradford Cemetery Company went into liquidation, the site was sold for £5 to a property developer, the buildings were demolished for the value of the materials, and much other fabric was sold, including kerbstones around graves. In 1984 the devastated and overgrown site was compulsorily

Modern artworks can be inserted sensitively into Victorian cemeteries, as with this glass path sculpture, made in 1988 by Catherine Yass, twining between monuments at The Rosary, Norwich.

purchased by Bradford Council, and a Friends group became a charity to administer and manage the site. The Undercliffe Cemetery Charity has reinstated the gateway, repaired monuments, cleared important overgrown areas and recreated a valuable resource for the city, used by schools for educational visits and by locals. Other groups of dedicated Friends are carrying out equally valuable work at neglected cemeteries, for example at Sheffield General, York, Tunbridge Wells, Arnos Vale in Bristol, and Highgate in London. Kensal Green and Brookwood still run commercially, but the railway lines and stations at the latter have gone, although vestiges of the platforms remain. At Brookwood a large area of pauper graves is now designated a Site of Special Scientific Interest for its Surrey heathland habitat and rare species.

Many cemeteries are well cared for by local authorities, for example Trowbridge, Wiltshire, and Tring, Hertfordshire, sometimes in partnership with Friends groups who offer advice and volunteers where staff is otherwise limited, such as at The Rosary, Norwich. Hospital and asylum cemeteries survive in varying condition, but military cemeteries, such as Netley and Aldershot, are usually well maintained. A perennial problem is the costly repair of sometimes vast chapel complexes when they have decayed, for example at Pudsey, Leeds, and Birkenhead. Many were demolished by local authorities in the mid-twentieth century, such as the pair at Beckett Street, Leeds, or one of the pair at Utley, West Yorkshire. Memorials become unstable without periodic maintenance and may be laid flat or even removed in large numbers if considered unsafe, rather than repaired and stabilised.

An acute need for burial space means that efforts are being made to identify ways in which Victorian cemeteries can be useful. Some have been damaged by burials in available spaces that were designed to remain open, such as paths, and others have had ground levels raised to allow new burials. The City of London Cemetery has pioneered work into the re-use of plots that have remaining spaces, which also brings funds for maintenance.

Cemeteries remain valuable community assets. They still commemorate the dead as a focal point for mourning and religious observance. In addition they provide local amenity, community focus, social uses for family and other history, wildlife habitats and horticultural collections, forming oases in urban environments. They remain valuable educational resources for architecture, ecology, history, geology and other subjects, as envisaged by Loudon. Some have their own written histories or booklets dedicated to these other aspects.

The National Association of Cemetery Friends brings together the various groups on their website and provides information on maintenance and restoration and help to start new groups. Funding may be available from the Heritage Lottery Fund, English Heritage, local authorities and charities. There is a positive future for Victorian cemeteries if communities value them and help to keep them alive.

FURTHER READING

The histories of some cemeteries have been written but may now be out of print. Local studies libraries are useful places to search for such publications.

The following selection highlights various aspects of the Victorian cemetery.

Barker, F. *Highgate Cemetery Victorian Valhalla*. John Murray, 1984.
Brooks, C. *Mortal Remains: The History and Present State of the Victorian and Edwardian Cemetery.* Wheaton, 1989.
Clark, C., and Davison, R. *In Loving Memory: The Story of Undercliffe Cemetery* [Bradford]. Sutton, 2004.
Clarke, J. M. *London's Necropolis: A Guide to Brookwood Cemetery*. Sutton, 2004.
Clarke, J. M. *The Brookwood Necropolis Railway.* Oakwood Press, 2006.
Curl, J. S. 'Nunhead Cemetery, London', *Transactions of the Ancient Monuments Society*, volume 22, 1977.
Curl, J. S. *Death and Architecture*. Sutton, 2000.
Curl, J. S. *Kensal Green Cemetery.* Phillimore, 2001.
Curl, J. S. *The Victorian Celebration of Death*. Sutton, 2002.
Geary, S. *Cemetery Design for Tombs and Cenotaphs*. 1840.
Horton, J. *Remote and Undisturbed: A Brief History of the Sheffield General Cemetery*. The Friends of the General Cemetery, 2001.
Hutt, C. *City of the Dead: The Story of Glasgow's Southern Necropolis.* Glasgow City Libraries and Archives, 1996.
Johnston, R. *Glasgow Necropolis Afterlives: Tales of Interments.* Johnstondesign, 2007.
Loudon, J. C. *On the Laying Out, Planting and Managing of Cemeteries.* Ivelet, 1981 (first published 1843).
Lovie, J. M. L. 'The Next Train is for Knowle Necropolis Only', *Warwickshire Gardens Trust Journal*, autumn 2003.
May, T. *The Victorian Undertaker.* Shire, 2003.
Meller, H. *London Cemeteries: An Illustrated Guide and Gazetteer*. Ashgate, fourth edition, 2008.
Murray, H. *This Garden of Death: The History of York Cemetery.* Friends of York Cemetery, 1991.

The Sanger Memorial in Margate Cemetery features a life-size circus horse in white marble and holds the remains of a famous Victorian circus family. John Sanger died in 1879. Note the horseshoe upturned in respect, and the elegant iron railing around the plot.

Pearson, L. F. *Discovering Famous Graves.* Shire, 1998.
Pearson, L. F. *Mausoleums.* Shire, 2002.
Robinson, W. *God's Acre Beautiful, or the Cemeteries of the Future.* 1880.
White, J., and Hodson, J. *Paradise Preserved: An Introduction to the Assessment, Evaluation, Conservation and Management of Historic Cemeteries.* English Heritage, 2007.

WEBSITES

British Association for Cemeteries in South Asia (BACSA): www.bacsa.org.uk
Brookwood Cemetery Limited: www.brookwoodcemetery.com
Brookwood Cemetery Society: www.tbcs.org.uk
English Heritage: www.englishheritage.org.uk/upload/pdf/cemeteries.pdf
Friends of Arnos Vale Cemetery, Bristol: www.arnosvalefriends.org.uk
Friends of Beckett Street Cemetery, Leeds: www.beckettstreetcemetery.org.uk
Friends of Highgate Cemetery: www.highgate-cemetery.org
Friends of Kensal Green Cemetery: www.kensalgreen.co.uk
Friends of Tower Hamlets Cemetery Park: www.towerhamletscemetery.org
Friends of West Norwood Cemetery: www.fownc.org
Indian Cemeteries: www.indian-cemeteries.org
National Federation of Cemetery Friends: www.cemeteryfriends.org.uk
Sheffield General Cemetery: www.gencem.org

Often the cemetery remains a pleasant environment for town-dwellers, such as this family walking through the first English garden cemetery, The Rosary, Norwich, on their way home from shopping.

PLACES TO VISIT

Most public cemeteries are open during the hours of daylight. The following cemeteries are mentioned in the text and cover a range of styles and periods.

GREAT BRITAIN
Arnos Vale Cemetery, Bath Road, Bristol BS4 3EW.
Brompton Cemetery, Old Brompton Road, London SW5.
Brookwood Cemetery, Cemetery Pales, Brookwood, Woking GU24 0BL.
City of London Cemetery, Aldersbrook Road, Manor Park, London E12.
Coventry Cemetery, London Road, Coventry CV4 7DF.
Flaybrick Memorial Gardens, Birkenhead.
Ford Park Cemetery, Ford Park Road, Plymouth PL4 6NT.
Glasgow Necropolis.
Golders Green Crematorium, Hoop Lane, London NW11.
Highgate Cemetery, Swain's Lane, London N6.
Jewish Cemetery, Glebe Road, Willesden, London NW10.
Kensal Green Cemetery, Harrow Road, London NW10.
Key Hill Cemetery, Icknield St, Birmingham B18 6PL.
Manchester Southern Cemetery, Barlow Moor Road, Manchester.
Newcastle General Cemetery, Jesmond Road, Newcastle.
Nunhead Cemetery, Linden Grove, London SE15.
Penzance Jewish Cemetery, Leskinnick Terrace, Penzance.
The Rosary Cemetery, Thorpe Road, Norwich.
St Bartholomew's Cemetery, Exeter.
St James's Cemetery, St James's Road, Liverpool.
Sheffield General Cemetery, Cemetery Avenue, Sheffield.
Stapenhill Cemetery, Burton upon Trent DE15 9AE.
Stoke Cemetery, Queens Road, Hartshill, Stoke on Trent ST4 7LH.
Trowbridge Cemetery, The Down, Trowbridge.
Undercliffe Cemetery, Undercliffe Lane, Bradford BD3 0QD.
Utley Cemetery, Skipton Road, Keighley BD20 6EJ.
York Cemetery, Cemetery Road, York YO10 5AJ.

OTHER COUNTRIES
Calcutta (Kolkata), India: South Park Street.
Dublin, Ireland: Glasnevin Cemetery.
Milan, Italy: Cimitero Monumentale.
New Orleans, USA: various.
Paris, France: Cimetière du Père-Lachaise.

INDEX

Page numbers in italic refer to illustrations

Adam, Robert 10
Aldershot (military) 37, 60
Augustus Frederick, Duke of Sussex 23
Bacup 32
Bahadoor, Raja Ramohun Roy 20
Barnett, J. & Birch, W. C. 39
Barnsley *3*, 41
Barry, T. D. 39
Bath, Abbey 29
Baud, Benjamin 19
Belfast, Clifton Street 10
Birkenhead (Flaybrick Memorial Garden) *30*, 33, 60
Birmingham:
  Brandwood End 54
  Key Hill 15, *15*, 18, 19, 23
Bishopwearmouth 54
Bonomi Jnr, Joseph 21
Bournemouth 54
Bradford, Undercliffe *26*, 31–2, *33*, 37, 41, *46*, *51*, 59–60
Bridlington 34, *38*, *40*, 41, 54
Bristol, Arnos Vale 16, 19–20, *19*, *20*, 21, 59, 60
Brookwood, Woking 6, 31, *32*, 35–7, *37*, *39*, 41, *44*, *46*, *47*, 49–53, *49*, *50*, *52*, 55–7, *55*, *56*, 60
Bunning, James 19, 21
Burton on Trent 38
Burton, R. 47
Butterfield family 47
Cadogan, Lord 46
Calcutta, India, South Park Street 9, *9*
Cambridge, Histon Road 24, *25*, 29
Cambridge, Mass, USA, Mount Auburn 16, 21
Carden, G. F. 10
Cheltenham 39, 41
Coventry, London Road 29, *29*
Davidson, Robert 35, 36
Dobson, John 19
Drummond, T. 13
Dublin, ROI, Glasnevin, Mount Prospect 16, 22, 23, *48*
Edinburgh, Calton Hill 10

Exeter:
  Higher *42*
  Jewish 9
  St Bartholomew's *18*, 20, 21, 22
Farrow, A. 49
Forrest, R. 13, 14
Foster, John 13
Gay, William 32, 33, 41
Geary, Stephen 19, 20, 23
George, E. & Yeates, A. 57
Glasgow:
  Crematorium 57
  Necropolis 16, *16*, 18, 22
Goodwin, F. 14
Gravesend 16, 19, 22, 23
Great Malvern 39
Harrogate *40*, *43*, *44*, *48*
Haywood, William 35, 36
Hendon 54
Hereford 39
Hosking, W. 21
Hume, David 10
Illingworth family 46
Jordans 8
Keith family 46
Kemp, Edward 33, 39
Knaresborough *38*, *43*, *48*
Knight, W. 39, 41
Lancaster 32
Leavesden 37
Leicester General 32
Leeds:
  Armley 18
  Beckett Street 18, *26*, *32*, 41, 42, *42*, 60
  Holbeck 18
  Horsforth *39*
  Lawnswood 32, 33
  Pudsey 32, 60
  Levi, Joseph 22
Liverpool:
  Anfield 33
  Crematorium 57
  Low Hill 13
  St James 13, *14*, 18
  Toxteth 32
London:
  Abney Park 17, 21, 45
  Alderney Road (Jewish) 8
  Brady Street (Jewish) 8
  Brockley *53*
  Brompton 17, 19
  Bunhill Fields 8
  Fulham (Jewish) 8–9

Golders Green Crematorium 57
Grand National, Primrose Hill 14–15, *14*
Great Northern 31, 34, 56
Hampstead 34
Hanwell 34
Highgate 17, *17*, 18, 19, 21, *21*, 22, *22*, 27, *39*, 59, 60
Hyde Park (pets) *45*
Kensal Green *12*, 13, 17, 21–3, 29, 60
Lauriston Road (Jewish) 8
Little Ilford (City of London) 34–6, *35*, *36*, 56, 60
Mortlake *47*
Necropolis and Mausoleum Company (LNC) 35
Nunhead 17, 19, 21, 22, 59
Putney Vale 34
St Pancras & Islington 34
Tower Hamlets 17, *17*
West Ham (Jewish) 34
West Norwood 17, 22, 28, *28*, *49*
Whitechapel (Jewish) 8
Willesden 34
Loudon, John Claudius 5, 14, 18, 24–9, *24*, 36, 51–5, 57, 58, 60
Manchester:
  Crematorium 57
  General 13, 15
Margate *61*
Menston, High Royds 37
Milan, Italy, Cimitero Monumentale *33*
Milner, H. E. 4, 34, 54
Netley (military) 37, 60
New Orleans, USA, Lafayette No. 1 10, *10*, *50*
Newcastle upon Tyne:
  General 15, 19
  Westgate Hill 13
Nicols family 46
Norwich, The Rosary 13, *48*, *49*, *59*, 60, *62*
Nottingham:
  Church Cemetery 29
  General 16

Onslow, Lord 35
Paris, France, Pere Lachaise 11, *11*, 15, 17, 18
Paxton, Joseph 29, 33
Pelham-Clinton, M. & E. *50*
Perkin and Backhouse 41
Penn, Jordans (Quaker) *8*, 9
Penzance (Jewish) 9
Plymouth:
  Hoe (Jewish) 9, 34
  (Jewish) *34*
  Stonehouse & Devonport (Ford Park Cemetery) *20*, *21*, 34
Princep, W. 20
Pritchett, J. P. 15
Poole 32, 41, *43*
Ramsay, David 19
Reading 19, 21, 22
Robinson, William 57
Rothschild, Evelina and Ferdinand 34
Ryde, Isle of Wight *53*
St Helens 33
St Louis, USA 10
Salviati, G. 51
Sanger family 61
Sheffield:
  City Road 41
  General 15, 21, 60
Shepherd, J. 13, 14
Shipston 39
Smirke, Sidney *32*, 39
Smith, A. 38, 41
Sophia, Princess 23
Southampton 18, 29
Stoke-on-Trent *4*
Strang, J. 13, 16, 24
Tavistock, Plymouth Road *53*
Thomas, William Broderick 36
Tite, William 22
Tring 60
Trowbridge *38*, *40*, 41, 60
Tubbs & Messer 39
Tunbridge Wells *7*, 60
Ulverston 41, *45*
Utley *40*, *44*, *47*, 60
Warlingham 37
Wadia family 47, 49
Wigan 32
Wilson, T. W. 45
Windsor, Frogmore 45
Woking, Crematorium 57
Wyatt, Matthew Digby 34
York 15, *15*, 16, 50, 57, 60